Digital
Photography
FOR
DUMMIES®
POCKET EDITION

Digital Photography FOR DUMMIES®

POCKET EDITION

by Mark Justice Hinton

author of *Digital Photography For Seniors For Dummies*

WILEY

Wiley Publishing, Inc.

Digital Photography For Dummies®, Pocket Edition

Published by
Wiley Publishing, Inc.
111 River Street
Hoboken, NJ 07030-5774

www.wiley.com

Copyright © 2011 by Wiley Publishing, Inc., Indianapolis, Indiana

Published by Wiley Publishing, Inc., Indianapolis, Indiana

Published simultaneously in Canada

For general information on our other products and services, please contact our Customer Care Department within the U.S. at 877-762-2974, outside the U.S. at 317-572-3993, or fax 317-572-4002.

For technical support, please visit www.wiley.com/techsupport.

Wiley also publishes its books in a variety of electronic formats. Some content that appears in print may not be available in electronic books.

ISBN: 978-0-470-94040-2

Manufactured in the United States of America

10 9 8 7 6 5 4 3 2

WILEY

Table of Contents

• •

Publisher's Acknowledgments

We're proud of this book; please send us your comments at http://dummies.custhelp.com. For other comments, please contact our Customer Care Department within the U.S. at 877-762-2974, outside the U.S. at 317-572-3993, or fax 317-572-4002. Some of the people who helped bring this book to market include the following:

Acquisitions and Editorial

Project Editor: Rebecca Senninger

Executive Editor: Steve Hayes

Copy Editor: Debbye Butler

Technical Editor: Dave Hall

Editorial Manager: Kevin Kirschner

Editorial Assistant: Amanda Graham

Sr. Editorial Assistant: Cherie Case

Cartoons: Rich Tennant
(www.the5thwave.com)

Composition Services

Project Coordinator: Kristie Rees

Layout and Graphics: Carl Byers, Carrie A. Cesavice

Proofreader: Susan Moritz

Publishing and Editorial for Technology Dummies

    Richard Swadley, Vice President and Executive Group Publisher

    Andy Cummings, Vice President and Publisher

    Mary Bednarek, Executive Acquisitions Director

    Mary C. Corder, Editorial Director

Publishing for Consumer Dummies

    Diane Graves Steele, Vice President and Publisher

Composition Services

    Debbie Stailey, Director of Composition Services

Introduction

Smile! Everybody say "cheese."

Photographs freeze a moment in time forever. Even an underexposed, out-of-focus photo may affect you as strongly as the finest photo art. Photographs fascinate and entertain. People like photos.

Whether you use a cell phone camera or a top-of-the-line professional model, the widespread availability of digital cameras has energized popular photography. At any moment — triumphant or embarrassing — you can be ready to capture the scene.

Some things about photography haven't changed with digital technology. Your pictures have a subject and a frame. You can compose your photo by following guidelines that go back further than anyone reading this book can remember. However, digital photography has brought a few radical changes to photography:

- ✔ Photos are immediately accessible and shareable — no more delayed gratification

- ✔ Photos last forever — digital never fades or curls

- ✔ Technology makes things easy that used to be impossible by enabling you to stop action and capture great details

The phrase *point and shoot* promises an ease of use that most digital cameras deliver. But this simplicity also brings new challenges, such as what to do with the 30,000 digital photos stashed on your hard drive.

About This Book

Taking good photographs does not require you to be exceptionally talented or studious. Neither should your photographs force your friends to yawn and make excuses to avoid looking at 300 similar shots from your vacation. The goal of this book is to help you enjoy taking pictures and to help you experiment with all the features of your camera, as well as to deal with your photos after the shot.

Whom This Book Is For

You may already have your first digital camera, or you may be ready to get a new one and are looking for some guidance on what type of digital camera to buy. Perhaps you want to take advantage of your camera's automatic functions, but you're curious about what else your camera can do. If you want to find out the essentials of digital photography — from choosing a camera to sharing your photos, and all the steps in between — this book is for you.

How This Book Is Organized

Digital Photography For Dummies, Pocket Edition is divided into six parts.

- ✔ Part I covers buying a digital camera and taking your first photos. You discover the features to look for in a new camera.
- ✔ Part II helps you set up your camera and get started taking basic and fun shots.
- ✔ Part III provides various composition techniques and tips.

✔ Part IV details fast and easy ways to transfer photos from your camera to your computer.

✔ Part V helps you understand exposure by explaining shutter speed, aperture, and ISO.

✔ Part VI provides ten tips for taking better photos.

Icons Used in This Book

The icons in this book point out especially important information that you don't want to miss:

Look for this icon for something extra, some suggestion you can easily put into practice right away.

Now and then, I want to remind you of something before you go on. I know you remember every word you read. I just want to be sure I didn't forget to mention something already.

When something pops up that could cause some trouble, such as "click Yes to delete all photos," I warn you about the consequences.

If I know of a good reference that covers a topic more completely than I can, I give you a heads-up about it with this symbol.

This icon marks particularly geeky information. This information isn't necessary to know to take great photos; read the text marked with this icon if you have an interest in how your camera takes those great photos.

Part I

Choosing Your Camera

. . . .

In This Part

▶ Choosing a camera type

▶ Focusing on features

▶ Opting for accessories

. . . .

Shopping for a digital camera is like choosing any other technical device, such as a computer or a car. You can carefully weigh multiple criteria considering expert reviews, or you can buy the blue one. As is true of any device, cameras have features that are more or less important, although people — especially enthusiasts — will disagree about the level of importance of a specific feature.

Your camera should be a good fit for you — not too small, not too large, and not too heavy. You want to feel comfortable carrying your camera, so that you always have it nearby, even when you don't expect to need it.

The camera you buy or have already may not do everything covered in this book. Or, it may do more than you discover here. However, most of the topics are of practical value to any photographer who doesn't already know them.

In this Part, I focus on the camera features you may want in your next camera. (I had to get that pun out of the way.) This information will help you navigate through ads and reviews to find the right fit.

Amazon (www.amazon.com) is a great source for reviews from real people who have used a particular product. For professional reviews of digital camera equipment, visit http://reviews.cnet.com/digital-cameras, www.dpreview.com, and www.steves-digicams.com. More sites are linked at my Web site: www.mjhinton.com/dp.

Picking a Camera Type

Before you pick up a camera, consider these three categories of digital cameras (just *cameras* from here on):

✔ **Point and Shoot (P&S)** cameras have a wide range of features that are covered in the section "Considering Camera Features." P&S cameras also range in size (from tiny to two-handed) and in price (from roughly $100 to $500).

You may find a bargain camera for less than $100, but look closely to be sure it doesn't have some unacceptable limit to the features discussed in this Part.

✔ **Digital Single Lens Reflex (DSLR)** cameras are based on the same design as that used for professional film cameras (SLR). In contrast to the *fixed* (unremovable) lens found on a P&S camera, you can change the lenses on a DSLR to suit the situation. You might switch to a macro lens for an extreme close-up, and then switch to a telephoto lens for a distant shot. Removable and exchangeable lenses distinguish DSLR from non-DSLR. DSLRs also give you more options for taking photos. Further, the size of DSLR image sensor promises better quality photos, especially for large prints.

✔ **High-end P&S cameras** bridge the gap between P&S and DSLRs, and include features otherwise normally found in DSLRs. Often, these cameras are called *superzooms* or *ultrazooms,* for that one feature. At one time, the industry called these "prosumer" (professional + consumer) and *bridge* (bridging the gap between types), though neither term caught on with consumers.

Table 1-1 shows a comparison of the three main types of digital cameras.

Table 1-1	Comparing Camera Types	
Style	*Cost*	*Description*
Basic P&S	$125 to $250	Easily slips into a pocket or small purse. Uses fixed lens and internal flash. Generally, few features, mostly automatic.
High-end P&S	$250 to $500	Has much of the power of a DSLR with the convenience of a point-and-shoot model. Usually has a high-range zoom lens. You can select between manual and multiple automatic modes.

(continued)

Table 1-1 *(continued)*		
Style	*Cost*	*Description*
DSLR	$500 to $5,000	Aimed at serious hobbyists and professional photographers. Many more automatic and manual options, requiring more experience. Extensive interchangeable lens and external flash options.

A note here about handy cellphone cameras: As cellphones become more sophisticated, their cameras improve, as well. Consider these the ultimate compact P&S. The added issue for cellphones is how do you get your photos out of the cellphone? It may be through a cable, a removable memory card, or via a data service added to your bill. If you're comparing cellphone cameras, most of the features covered in this Part are still relevant to you.

Point & Shoot (P&S)

With cameras, size matters. Most compact cameras that fit easily into your pocket are P&S. You may want a compact camera that is easy to carry and that you can pull out of your pocket for impromptu snapshots, like the one in Figure 1-1. Keep in mind that you may not be able to capture details from far away or extremely close up. In turn, fewer features generally make a camera easier to use.

Figure 1-1: A compact P&S.

Within the P&S type, there is a wide range of size from compact (pocket-sized) to large-bodied, but size doesn't always equate to features. High-end features may appear in any size of camera. Still, the high-end P&S cameras with long zoom lenses look a lot like DSLRs, as well as old-school film cameras. These cameras are too large for a normal-size pocket. See Figure 1-2.

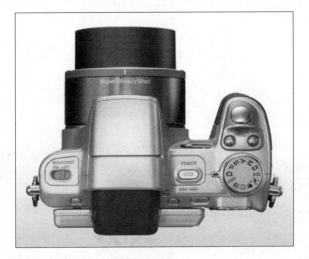

Figure 1-2: High-end P&S are larger than compacts.

If size or cost doesn't matter, the key feature to determine whether you want a compact P&S or a high-end P&S is how much zoom factor you want. A zoom lens has adjustable focus from near (wide) to far (telephoto). A zoom lets you get closer to a distant subject and fill the frame. Zoom is measured in factors: 3x is three times closer than the wide angle lens; 10x is ten times closer. Most compact P&S cameras have a maximum of 5x or 8x. High-end P&S start at 10x — 30x is the current extreme. Figure 1-3 shows the same scene using a zoom ranging from 1x (no zoom) to 12x. At 20x, the stop sign would nearly fill the frame.

The appeal of a long zoom may be obvious (getting really close to a distant subject without moving). A zoom of 10x or more is great for an outdoors photographer. There are issues with zooms to keep in mind:

✔ **The longer the zoom the greater the odds of shakiness or blurriness.** You need good image stabilization and very bright light for handheld shots — or a tripod.

✔ **A long zoom makes a high-end P&S bulky and expensive.** On high-end P&S, zooms lurch a bit (sometimes noisily) between zoom levels, whereas DSLRs zoom smoothly and quietly (qualities you pay for).

1x

3x

5x

12x

Figure 1-3: Zoom from wide to telephoto.

A superzoom (beyond 10x) isn't for everyone. However, if you buy a compact P&S, get one with a zoom between 5x and 10x, if you can.

Zoom can be optical or digital (or both). Digital zoom automatically crops the photo, lowering the resolution of the picture. The quality of a digital zoom rarely matches optical zoom. Ignore digital zoom when comparing two cameras.

A rational person would assume all 12x cameras zoom 20 percent farther or closer than all 10x cameras. That is not necessarily so because the x refers to the wide angle (near) focal length of the lens for that specific camera. For this reason, to accurately compare two cameras' lenses, you need to know the range from wide to telephoto. This range often appears on the front of the lens. For example, a compact camera with a range from 5mm to 25mm has a 5x zoom. A high-end P&S ranging from 5mm to 100mm has a 20x zoom.

Technical specifications and reviews often convert zoom to film-camera 35 millimeter equivalents. (This is more familiar to film and DSLR photographers.) The compact camera referred to in the preceding paragraph ranges from 30mm to 150mm (5x), whereas the high-end P&S range is 28mm to 560mm (20x).

Digital Single Lens Reflex (DSLR)

As noted earlier, DSLRs have removable lenses. However, there are other reasons to consider buying a DSLR:

✔ **The image sensor is larger.** A larger sensor doesn't necessarily mean larger photos, but better quality photos due to improved light-gathering and processing.

✔ **Overall speed — startup and shooting — is usually higher.** P&S users often experience a lag between pressing the shutter and capturing the image, during which time a subject may move.

✔ **You have the capability to shoot in the RAW format.** Enthusiasts prefer RAW for processing photos in powerful photo-editing programs such as Adobe Photoshop.

The body of a DSLR determines most of the features of that camera, although some designs put features such as image stabilization into the lens instead of the body. Further, the camera body determines the lenses you can use. (Although, indeed, there are adapter rings that allow a camera from one manufacturer to use the lenses from another, but that's pretty hardcore.)

Figure 1-4 shows the type of DSLR camera that a professional photographer might use.

Photo credit: www.sxc.hu

Figure 1-4: A DSLR.

Your DSLR may come with a general purpose lens —
double-check before you buy, because some prices
are for a body only. Regardless, most DSLR users
have more than one lens, including the following:

- ✔ A short, versatile **wide-angle lens** suitable for
  portraits and landscapes.

- ✔ A **macro** lens for extreme close-ups.

- ✔ A **zoom** lens to range from near to far subjects.

- ✔ A **telephoto,** instead of a zoom, with a fixed
  length for very distant subjects.

- ✔ A **fish-eye lens,** an extreme wide-angle that dis-
  torts pictures in a way similar to a peephole on
  an apartment door.

Figure 1-5 shows a few lenses.

Photo credit: iStockphoto.com

Figure 1-5: Lenses give DSLRs versatility.

Filters screw to the end of DSLR lenses to protect the lens, filter ultraviolet light (UV), reduce
water or glass reflections (polarizing), and more.

Considering Camera Features

Some camera features are universal, whereas others vary with the manufacturer. For example, every camera has a button you press to snap the shot (the shutter release). Where that shutter button is located and how hard you press it varies from camera to camera.

Every camera has the following features:

- ✔ The **lens** focuses the scene. The lens could be plastic but is usually glass; also, it may be immobile or may extend from the camera body when you turn the camera on or adjust focus.

- ✔ The **lens cover** protects the lens. The cover may slide automatically or detach manually as a lens cap. (Don't lose it.)

- ✔ The **shutter release button** usually has two steps. Press partly to set the focus and other automatic settings and fully to take the picture. Smile. Click!

- ✔ The **viewfinder (VF)** lets you put your eye next to the camera to compose a shot. The area you see in the VF may be a little more or less than the area of the picture. The viewfinder may be optical (clear glass or plastic) or **electronic (EVF)**. An EVF displays useful information about camera settings but may be hard to see in bright light.

- ✔ A **liquid crystal display (LCD)** shows the scene and camera settings before you take the picture. A large (at least 3 inches), bright LCD is great for viewing pictures after you take them and for dealing with menus and other settings. Some LCDs are touchscreens enabling you to use menus with your finger. Some LCDs fold out from the back of the camera, allowing you to hold the camera high or low for a different perspective.

Some cameras have only an LCD, not a VF. I recommend you buy a camera that has an EVF. Without it, you have to hold the camera at arms' length to compose your shot, which is hard to hold stable. Further, most LCDs are hard to see in bright light.

✔ **Viewfinder/LCD toggle** switches between an electronic viewfinder (EVF) and the larger LCD display, which is best for menus, macros, and reviewing your pictures.

✔ **Review or playback control** shows the pictures you've already taken on the LCD or EVF.

✔ An **image sensor** receives the incoming image, which is processed into a stored file. The image sensor is likely to be a charge-coupled device (CCD) or complementary metal-oxide semiconductor (CMOS). Either technology is satisfactory for most photographers. As noted in the "Digital Single Lens Reflex" section, the larger issue is the size of the image sensor: Compact P&Ss have the smallest sensors, whereas DSLRs have much larger sensors. (In comparing two DSLRs, you may want to compare sensor size and reputation among professionals and enthusiasts.) Image sensor size matters most in advanced editing and printing photos.

✔ **Batteries** power all the camera functions. Some cameras require a special battery; some use generic batteries.

Buy and carry extra batteries. If you want your photographic endeavors to be a little greener, use rechargeables and travel with a recharger.

✔ A **storage or memory card** holds your pictures. Most cameras have built-in storage, but that is surely too limited. See the "Removable memory cards" section, later in this Part, for more about storage.

✔ A **mode dial** turns to enable you to switch among settings for different conditions, such as sporting events or nighttime (see Figure 1-6).

Figure 1-6: Use the Mode dial to change camera settings.

✔ A **Function dial** provides buttons necessary in menus, such as up, right, down, and left. The center of the function dial is a raised button for OK or Enter. Most cameras assign additional functions to these five controls when you are not using a menu, such as the self-timer and the flash control.

Look for reviews on the Web that describe and critique the menus used in a camera you're considering. Once you have a camera, spend some time exploring your camera's menus and documentation so that you have a better understanding of how to get the most out of your camera.

✔ **Flash control** turns the flash on or off.

✔ **Self-timer** lets you jump into the picture before it's taken.

✔ All but the most basic cameras also have a **flash.** Some flashes pop up or out automatically; some are controlled manually.

You may find any of these additional controls on a camera:

✔ A **dedicated video control** on a few cameras lets you start and stop video with one button. Most cameras require you to switch to Video mode with the mode wheel and start and stop with the shutter button.

✔ **Image stabilization** reduces shakiness or blurring and is critical for zoomed photos and some low-light photos.

✔ **Focus control** lets you set a specific distance between the camera and the subject to override autofocus. This is most useful when autofocus is unreliable, especially in low light.

✔ **Burst mode** lets you hold down the shutter button to capture as many photos as possible in rapid succession, which is especially useful in sports or with wildlife.

✔ **Bracketing mode** takes multiple shots when you press the shutter button, but adjusts each shot's exposure slightly. This is useful in situations where the camera may be wrong about automatic settings or you may be wrong about manual settings.

✔ **Face or smile detection** assures the camera focuses on faces. Newer technology can actually delay the exposure until everyone in the photo is smiling. Go ahead, smile. There is no sincerity filter.

✔ **Panorama mode** prompts you to slowly pan your camera from side to side as the camera shoots multiple shots and stitches them into one wide exposure.

✔ **GPS (Global Positioning System)** tags each photo with the global coordinates of that location (latitude and longitude). This process is called *geotagging.*

GPS built into a camera is still rare, though it is becoming more common. More common are programs for adding geotags manually or by using tracks recorded by a separate GPS device.

✔ **Remote controls** are rare, but handy for tripod-mounted shots or for playback and slide shows.

High-end P&Ss and DSLRs have even more specialty features and capabilities.

Exposure Settings or Modes

There is more to taking a picture than pointing and shooting. In addition to a fully automatic mode that controls everything, most cameras feature *scene modes* that automatically set the camera for certain conditions. As you compare cameras, you may want to consider specific scene modes they provide, especially those on the Mode dial, which will be the easiest to access.

The purpose of these scene modes is to make it easy to adjust the camera to different conditions. The camera settings required to photograph a tiny flower are different from those required for a mountain or a person running. Some newer cameras analyze the scene and choose scene modes automatically.

Recent cameras offer such a huge number of specialty modes (for example, *fireworks* and *party,* whatever that means) that the sheer number of scene modes may not matter in your buying decision.

Look for symbols or letters that represent these modes around the Mode dial (refer to Figure 1-6). In some cases, you select scene modes through a menu. Consider these common scene modes:

✔ **Landscape** mode sets the focus to infinity; look for a mountain-like triangular symbol indicating this mode.

✔ **Macro** mode, signified by a flower symbol, sets the focus very, very close — a fraction of an inch.

✔ **Sports** mode takes very fast pictures to freeze the action. You may see a golfer or a runner as the symbol for this mode, although a soccer player seems more appropriate.

✔ **Nighttime** mode (look for a crescent moon or a star) adjusts for low light.

✔ **Video** mode turns your camera into a camcorder. The symbol may be a piece of film with sprocket holes along the edge or a reel-to-reel projector (both of which are now rather antiquated symbols). Press the shutter button to start recording a video and again to stop.

Beyond the preset scene modes, high-end P&S and DSLR cameras typically include the following functions for controlling camera functions:

- ✔ **Aperture Priority (A or Av, for Aperture Value)**
  lets you control the size of the lens opening
  (aperture); the camera adjusts the shutter
  speed. A bigger aperture lets in more light,
  which is best in low-light conditions, but has a
  narrower *depth-of-field* (how deep an area is in
  focus). A smaller aperture lets in less light but
  has a deeper depth-of-field, which is best for a
  landscape on a bright day. Aperture values
  often appear stamped on the camera lens.

- ✔ **Shutter Priority (S or Tv, for Time Value)** is the
  opposite of Aperture Priority: You control the
  speed of the shutter; the camera controls the
  aperture. Capturing action requires a faster/
  higher shutter speed. A slower shutter speed is
  appropriate for low light.

When you compare two cameras, if all other
things are equal, the one with the wider range of
both aperture values and shutter values may be
the better camera (or lens), if you intend to
learn the subtleties of controlling settings. See
Part II for information on controlling these
settings.

- ✔ **Manual (M)** enables you to set both the aperture and the shutter speed. Manual control
  enables exquisite control over the exposure, but
  requires experience and experimentation.

Examining Image Size and Storage

Digital images are made up of dots (*pixels,* which is
short for *picture elements*). More pixels in an image
mean more dots. These dots are bits of information,
such as color and brightness, about each spot in the
larger image.

Each picture you take is stored in the camera as a file.
Bigger files store more information, increasing your
editing and printing options. Three features combine
to determine just how many pictures you can store in
your camera: the *resolution* of your images; the file
format in which your camera stores your photos; and
the type of memory card on which you are storing
your photos. I discuss these three features in the following sections.

For the greatest flexibility, buy a camera with
high resolution. Set the resolution to the max.
Choose the format that stores the most information (biggest files). Buy the largest memory card
the camera supports.

Image resolution

A *pixel* is a dot of information about color and brightness. Your computer screen may be 1,024 pixels wide
by 768 pixels high — 786,432 pixels or .78 *megapixels*
(MP — millions of pixels) in area. Consider an image
that is 800 pixels wide and 600 pixels high (480,000
pixels in area). That image doesn't fill your screen.
Printed on the average personal computer printer,
this hypothetical photo is a little bigger than a
postcard.

If you want a bigger photo on-screen or on paper, you
need more pixels. The maximum number of pixels per
photo is a camera's *resolution*. The more pixels in an
image — the higher the resolution — the bigger you
can print the image. You set the image resolution
through your camera's setup menus up to the maximum the camera supports.

The ideal resolution for you depends on what you plan to do with the photo. Most of the photos displayed on Web sites are 1,024 by 768 pixels or smaller — less than 1 MP. An e-mailed photo might be even smaller, unless the recipient wants to print it. If you'll never print that photo at all — or at least never larger than at the standard print size of 4 x 6 inches — isn't 2 MP enough?

To answer that question, consider that you'll surely want to *crop* photos occasionally to eliminate some of the outer portions of the image in order to draw attention to a specific detail. The more megapixels you have, the smaller the portion of the original you can crop to and still have something to see and print. Even if you never expect to print especially large photos, having a 16 MP camera means that you can print large if you want, and it gives you the capability to crop your photo to a tiny area and still have a decent-size image.

If you plan to edit your photos, the more pixels available, the better.

Figure 1-7 shows a photo of a Cooper's hawk soaring. Figure 1-8 shows the hawk cropped from Figure 1-7. The original photo's resolution is 3,072 wide (W) x 2,304 high (H) — not quite 8 MP. The cropped area is 853W x 586H. If the original had been a lower resolution, none of the detail of the hawk would be visible cropped. That picture would be made up of too few dots, resulting in a blotchy, pixelated effect. As it is, Figure 1-8 is too small to blow up into a large print.

3,072 (W) x 2,304 (H)

Figure 1-7: The subject is a small part of the original photo.

853 (W) x 586 (H)

Figure 1-8: Cropping eliminates part of the picture to emphasize the subject.

Can you have too many megapixels? Sorta. A deep consideration of megapixels requires returning to the image sensor, which receives the light that becomes the photo. Imagine a compact P&S with 12 MP and a DSLR with 12 MP. The sensor on the compact P&S is much smaller — less than 25 percent as large — so those pixels are small and packed together, whereas they are larger on the DSLR. The smaller sensor is subject to more electrical interference ("noise") resulting in less satisfactory images, especially in low light or blown up large. Most compact P&Ss top out at 10 to 12 MP, whereas DSLRs may have 18 MP or more.

There is another negative aspect to lots of megapixels: The resulting file size is larger, taking more space on the memory card or on your hard drive and creating bigger attachments to e-mail, as well as making files slower to copy. This is why your camera's setup menu enables you to choose lower resolutions if you want to store more pictures per memory card. Better to buy a larger card than sacrifice pixels.

File formats

You need to know how big each photo is before you know how many photos you can save per gigabyte. Digital cameras store photos and videos in various file formats that use file extensions such as .jpg and .mov. Some formats produce larger files, which take up more space on your memory card. A larger picture takes more storage space and more time to save and copy, but may produce better photos.

The available formats are determined by the camera manufacturer. If you have a choice, use your camera's setup menus to select the file format you want to use.

   ✔ The **JPEG** format (Joint Photographic Experts Group) is the most widely used in cameras and on computers. It is a very logical choice for cameras.

You may be able to select among JPEG types, such as Basic or Fine. JPEG compresses files and you want the least compression — the finest — available.

✔ The **RAW** format (not an acronym) is very popular on DSLRs. Unfortunately, there are different RAW formats and none is as universally recognized as JPEG, which complicates editing and sharing these photos. However, RAW stores all the information the sensor can capture, whereas JPEG mathematically compresses some data that might be useful in editing or printing — *might* being the operative word, so don't obsess over this.

✔ Video file formats include **MPEG** (Motion Picture Experts Group), **MOV** (Apple's QuickTime), and **AVI** (Audio Video Interleave). More and more cameras offer high-definition (HD) video suitable for HDTV.

The more important video is to you, the more attention you should pay to video format and resolution, as well as camera connections such as HDMI for connecting to HDTV.

Removable memory cards

The more gigabytes your memory card holds, the more pictures you can store on it. The type of card you use is determined by your camera; however, you can probably buy the card your camera requires in various storage capacities (more or fewer gigabytes). Table 1-2 shows a comparison of card types. (A *gigabyte,* which the numbers in the middle column refer to, is equal to one billion bytes.)

Table 1-2	Types of Memory Cards	
Media	*Gigabytes*	*Description*
CompactFlash (CF) card	1, 2, 4, 8, 16	Largest in apparent size (not necessarily storage size) and the oldest card type still in use.
Secure Digital (SD) card	1, 2, 4, 8	More compact than CF; most common mini and micro sizes used in other, smaller devices or in cameras using an adapter.
Secure Digital High Capacity (SDHC)	4, 8, 16, 32	Newer version of SD card; faster, smaller but larger capacity. The Micro SD is the size of a fingernail. Class 6 is currently the fastest version.
XD picture	1, 2	Used primarily by Olympus.
Memory Stick card	1, 2, 4, 8	Used with Sony cameras and Sony devices; Pro (greater capacity), Duo (small form), and Pro Duo (more capacity in a smaller package) versions are also in use.

The cards shown in Table 1-2 are available in various speeds. Slower-speed cards may be less expensive than faster cards but can affect camera performance. The slower the card, the longer it takes the camera to read and write to the card. Card speed affects how many photos you can take per second. Card speed may affect the frames per second (fps) for video. (Lower fps results in jerkier video.) However, don't buy

a faster or higher-capacity card without determining whether your camera can take advantage of it.

Figure 1-9 shows the following items from left to right:

🖊 An adapter that makes it possible to plug the
Memory Stick Pro into a computer, a digital
photo frame, or a suitable TV.

🖊 Memory Stick Pro, used by Sony cameras.
Nearly three times larger than the Micro SD, this
Memory Stick Pro has half the storage capacity.

🖊 A tiny 4GB Micro SD card. SD cards are the
most commonly used cards, except as noted in
Table 1-2.

🖊 An adapter that enables the Micro SD to fit a
camera that requires the older and larger style
SD card. There is also an adapter for the in-
between-size Mini-SD. Most Micro SD cards
come with a larger adapter.

🖊 An adapter that makes it possible to plug an SD
card into a computer, a digital photo frame, or a
TV with a USB port.

Strictly speaking, you can save a limited number
of photos directly to your camera's built-in
memory. Then, you can use the cable that came
with your camera to transfer the images directly
to your PC. However, this severely limits how
many pictures you can take before you have to
move them to your computer. Insert a compati-
ble memory card, and your camera uses it automatically. For more information about
transferring photos to your PC, see Part IV.

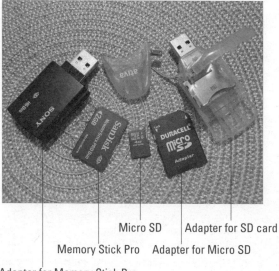

Micro SD   Adapter for SD card
Memory Stick Pro   Adapter for Micro SD
Adapter for Memory Stick Pro

Figure 1-9: Two memory storage cards surrounded by adapters.

Accessorizing Your Camera

You start with a camera, but you end up with more stuff. Gear gathers more gear. You may end up with all of these things, as you need them, of course.

> ✔ **Extra batteries and charger:** Whether your camera uses a special proprietary battery or generic batteries, you don't want to run out of power. Have backup batteries and practice

switching batteries with one eye on the scene. For car trips, you may need an adapter to plug your charger into the DC connection. For foreign travel, you may need an adapter for local outlets.

✔ **Extra memory cards:** In one outing, you may not shoot enough pictures to fill your memory card. Still, the longer you go without moving those pictures off the camera, the more you need an extra card. For long trips, you also have to consider what happens if a card fails — they do sometimes.

✔ **Extra camera:** Seriously. Again, in a travel situation, what happens if your camera fails or gets lost or stolen? Even without that concern, if your primary camera is a high-end P&S or DSLR, there are times when that just stands out too much and a compact P&S would be very handy.

✔ **Tripod:** By attaching your camera to a tripod, you make the camera extremely stable for long zoom shots, shots in low light or at night, and for self-portraits, including group shots you jump into. A good tripod collapses small enough to carry comfortably and expands easily but securely to a height you don't have to bend over for. (A flip-out LCD on the camera helps here.) Ideally, the tripod head turns up or down and left or right and locks in a position.

Everyone needs a pocket-size tripod for quick self-portraits and group shots. Some small tripods wrap around or clip to objects for extra stability.

✔ **Monopod:** Like a hiking stick or ski pole with a connector at the top, a monopod is easier to move than a tripod, but a monopod is much less stable.

✔ **External flash:** Primarily an option for DSLR, an external flash triggered by the camera gives you more lighting options.

✔ **Reflectors:** With any camera, you can use reflectors to change the light on the subject, particularly to remove shadows. Reflectors may be large squares, ovals, or umbrella shaped, in shades of white or gray. Position in front of and to one side of the subject to reflect natural light or a flash.

✔ **Extra lenses:** Another DSLR option, particularly Macro and Telephoto or Zoom. One lens is never enough (except for P&S users).

✔ **Lens filters:** Uncommon for P&S, filters protect lenses (neutral filter) and usually modify the light in various ways, such as a polarizing filter to reduce haze and intensify blue sky and water.

✔ **Camera bag:** You may be thinking "suitcase" by now. Consider two bags. Get one small padded bag for your camera plus extra batteries and cards to hang from your shoulder or your belt. Use another for everything else — perhaps one with wheels.

 When you take a trip, think carefully about what gear you can't live without and how to transport it safely.

✔ **Cables:** If you intend to connect your camera directly to a computer or TV, you need cables for that (they should come with the camera). A few cameras have power cords.

✔ **Card reader or adapter:** Instead of connecting your camera directly to a computer or TV, you can remove the card and put it into a card reader or a USB adapter, which turns the card into a flash drive.

✔ **Computer:** You do not have to have a computer to take and enjoy photos. You can do a lot with just your camera's LCD. You may be able to connect your camera or card to a TV. You can insert the card into a digital photo frame. You can take your camera to a photo printer. Still, a computer gives you much more, enabling you to organize, edit, and share your photos. For travel, a small laptop or netbook is ideal.

✔ **Printer:** There are portable printers, but here I'm thinking about a printer for your home computer.

You're well acquainted with the camera strap most photographers use to hang their cameras around their necks. Compacts usually come with a lightweight wrist strap. You may be able to add a neck strap to your compact. For any size camera, consider a wrist strap sturdy enough to keep your camera safe and close at hand.

Part II

Fast and Easy Picture Taking

. . . .

In This Part

▶ Setting up your camera for the first time

▶ Getting good-quality images

▶ Examining your camera's preset modes

▶ Finding the best light for your subject

▶ Having some fun with your camera

▶ Checking out the photos you've taken

. . . .

*W*ith camera in hand, you're ready to shoot. In this chapter, you discover enough to jump into using your camera with confidence. Before your first shot, set the image quality and get a sense of your camera's many automatic modes. Check out a few tips about light — photography is all about light and dark. And then take some fun shots before you review the photos on your camera's LCD.

Because of differences between camera makes and models, some setting names and locations may be different from what you find here. Be sure to have your camera's user manual handy, and remember that nothing beats getting out there and running your camera through its paces. Try every setting, take a shot, and see what happens: That's really the only way to truly feel comfortable with your camera.

Setting Up Your New Camera

Out of the box, there are a few things you need to do just one time with a new camera. Follow these steps:

1. **When you get your camera, lay out all the items that came with it and confirm that you received everything you expected from the packing slip, box label, or ad.**

    If your camera came with specific step-by-step instructions for setting up the camera for its first use, follow those steps instead of the steps here before you take your first picture.

2. **Remove all packaging, including tape.**

    Store this material until you're sure you won't need to return your camera to the seller.

3. **If your camera has a neck or wrist strap, thread the strap ends through the slots on either side of the camera body.**

    Take care to attach the strap securely. Test it gently. You don't want your camera to fall off this strap.

4. **Install the memory card, if you have one (see Part I for information about memory or storage cards).**

    Look for a small cover on the bottom of the camera or either side. Many cameras have one cover for both memory card and batteries, as shown in Figure 2-1. Open the door by pushing or sliding the cover. With your thumb on the label side of the memory card and any exposed metal contacts away from you, gently insert the card into the card slot. If you meet resistance, pull the card out and turn your hand to try inserting the card the other way. The card should slide in easily and stay in. (It may click in place.) Do not force the card. Close the memory card slot cover.

Battery   Memory card

Figure 2-1: The memory card and battery may share a compartment and cover.

To remove a memory card, with the cover open, push the card in slightly, and when you release, it should pop out. Never pull or pry a card out.

 Never install or remove a memory card while the camera is on. You could lose photos or damage the card.

5. **Install the battery or batteries.**

   Look for a small compartment on the bottom or side of the camera. Open the door by pushing or sliding the cover. If the battery is rectangular, put your thumb on the label and gently push it in — the battery will go in only one way. If your camera uses two or four standard batteries, look for an indication of which end goes in for each battery. (The standard batteries don't all go in the compartment facing the same way; they alternate.)

6. **Locate the lens cover.**

   If it's a separate piece, leave it unattached for now. If the lens cover clips in place, remove the cover before you turn on the camera. (In some camera models, when you turn on the camera, the lens will strike the lens cover if you forget to remove it.) If the cover slides, gently sliding it may turn the camera on. Don't force the lens cover off or on.

   Some lens caps come with a thin string you can slip through a hole in the lens cap and another hole in the camera body or around the camera strap to keep the cap with the camera. When the camera is off, the lens cap should be in place.

7. **Turn on the camera if moving the lens cover didn't do that automatically.**

   Look for a message on the LCD or in the viewfinder.

   The camera may automatically ask for the current date and time, which will be recorded with each photograph. Enter that information using the up and down buttons to change numbers and use the right and left buttons to move to different parts of the date and time. These buttons are usually arranged around the outside of a circular button. After you've selected the current date and time, press the center button to set the changes.

8. **Take a picture of anything.**

   Go ahead. You know you want to.

9. **If your camera came with a CD or DVD, you can install that software on a computer later.**

   The software may include a program for viewing and editing your pictures. See Part IV for information about copying pictures from camera to computer.

 Stick an address label (plus your phone number and e-mail address) onto your camera in the hope that someone will return it to you if you lose it. I also put a copy of this info on a small label I stick to the battery of my camera.

Setting Image Quality

You want to take great photos, so make sure your camera is working with you. Set the image quality to yield the best photos and to give you maximum flexibility in editing and printing.

Image quality can be affected by two different settings: resolution and file format (both introduced in Part I). For maximum flexibility after you've taken a photo, you want the highest resolution your camera is capable of, although that does produce the largest files. That means fewer photos will fit on your memory card. So you need to find a balance between resolution and file size. Use your camera's setup menu to see what options are available.

Figure 2-2 shows a sample Image Quality menu with quality options listed from highest to lowest (top to bottom) — and, in effect, file size from largest to smallest.

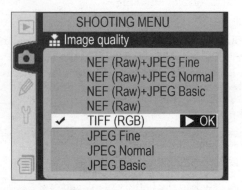

Figure 2-2: Choose a setting from the image quality menu.

Cameras support at least one of the following three file formats:

✔ **JPEG/JPG:** This is the most widely used format for photographs. After all, JPEG originates with the Joint Photographic *Experts* Group. JPEG is designed to compress images in a very clever way by calculating what information you won't miss. JPEG compression varies by percentage, although most cameras don't specify a percentage. In Figure 2-2, notice the two options: JPEG Fine (which uses little or no compression) and JPEG Basic (which uses greater compression but probably still results in adequate quality except for the highest grade and largest prints). In between the two in size and quality is JPEG Normal.

If file size isn't an issue, you want JPEG with the least compression. On the menu shown in Figure 2-2, for example, you would choose JPEG Fine.

✔ **TIFF/TIF:** This *tagged image file format* is an old format originally used for scanned images. There are variations on TIFF, including some with compression, but it is usually a *lossless* file type — no data is removed during compression — and files are large, which results in higher-quality images but fewer photos per memory card. Although TIFF is common on computers, it is less common on cameras.

✔ **RAW:** This is the newest format and can vary among cameras. The goal of RAW is to capture more information — everything the image sensor sees. RAW might include additional copies of the image with different exposures or formats, such as RAW + JPEG.

So, is RAW best and JPEG worst? Not necessarily. Remember that you will be viewing these pictures on your computer, attaching them to e-mail, uploading them to the Web, and editing them for hours. Every program for working with or viewing photos handles JPEG easily. Only the latest software handles RAW. If you e-mail a huge RAW file to a friend, she may not be able to see it. JPEG gets points for longevity and ease of use, as well as smaller file size.

So, JPEG is best, right? Hold on. JPEG is lossy — JPEG compresses by throwing away data. If you repeatedly edit and save the same JPEG photo, you compress it more and more, eventually substantially degrading the quality.

For the record, Adobe, the maker of Photoshop and other photo editors, has created a RAW variant called

Digital Negative (DNG). Microsoft has its own format, HD Photo. The question remains as to whether camera makers will adopt these formats.

Relying on Automatic Mode

Regardless of which model of camera you have, there is an automatic mode that manages all options for taking pictures. You still have to aim the camera and press the shutter release, but the camera does everything else for you. This mode is truly point-and-shoot.

Look for a mode dial, dedicated buttons, or menu options. Figure 2-3 shows a mode dial set to A for Automatic. Your camera may show Auto or a camera icon. This control will be highlighted differently from all others.

Some cameras have a separate *Easy* setting, which displays less info on the LCD and may limit other options. It's your choice, but I think you want the information and options, eventually.

The following steps guide you through taking your first photo with Automatic mode:

1. **Set the Mode dial or button to Automatic mode.**

   In Automatic mode, your camera makes all the decisions.

2. **Compose your shot in the viewfinder or LCD screen.**

3. **Press the shutter button halfway down to give your camera a moment to focus.**

   This takes a fraction of a second, in most cases. You may see a green indicator on the LCD or

electronic viewfinder (EVF). You may see on-
screen information about the settings the camera
is automatically using.

4. **Press the shutter button the rest of way to capture the image.**

   Writing the captured file to the memory card takes
   a fraction of a second — longer for bigger files.

5. **Repeat Steps 1–4 as many times as you like.**

See the section "Reviewing Photos and Videos on
Your Camera," later in this Part, for information about
seeing the photos you've taken.

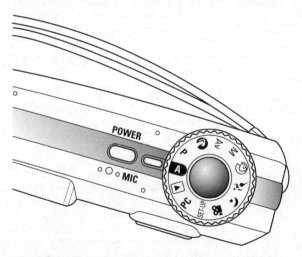

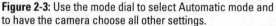
Figure 2-3: Use the mode dial to select Automatic mode and
to have the camera choose all other settings.

Although Auto mode will serve you well 90 percent of the time or more, you do have other options. You can guide the camera toward the right settings using scene modes (covered in the next section) or you may be able to take more direct control over settings, depending on your camera.

Using Preset Scene Modes

Automatic mode does it all, of course. Don't be afraid to operate on Automatic — even professionals do. However, you will surely shoot in conditions in which other modes produce better pictures. Your camera probably has various scene modes that configure the camera for specific shooting conditions. Using these modes is easy and may produce better pictures than leaving the camera in Auto mode — you just have to experiment.

Auto mode actually selects specific scene modes automatically. You may see an icon for the selected mode on the screen. Choose the scene mode yourself if Auto mode makes the wrong choice.

Some cameras have separate options on the mode dial for the most important scene modes. Most cameras have a Scene (or SCN) setting on the mode dial, which allows you to use a menu to specify the scene mode. Not all cameras have the same scene modes. Further, names and symbols for scenes vary between cameras. Consider a few common scene modes (names may vary on different cameras):

✔ **Portrait** sets the camera to focus on and expose the subject and not the background. The symbol is often a head and shoulders icon.

✔ **Landscape** sets the camera to focus and expose the entire scene. You may have separate modes for special landscapes such as beach or snow, both of which are very bright. This symbol is usually two or more triangles, meant to look like mountains.

 ✔ **Twilight** sets the camera for very low light. You may also have twilight portrait mode for portraits in low light and night mode for the darkest scenes. This symbol may be a crescent moon or a moon and star.

 ✔ **Sports** sets the camera focus on and freezes fast action. This symbol may look like a stylized runner or soccer player.

✔ **Other special modes** include fireworks, underwater, even food. Some cameras have dozens of special modes, many of which probably produce similar settings.

By selecting a specific scene mode (for example, Landscape), you guide the camera toward settings appropriate for the scene you're shooting.

 Take lots of pictures. Take the same picture several times, switching modes.

Shedding Some Light on Your Subject

Nothing is more important than light in photography. Or is darkness more important? In fact, a photo captures light and dark, as well as color. Photographers use numerous terms to describe the interplay of light and dark, such as exposure, contrast, and brightness.

Your camera's scene modes are preset for certain conditions of light and darkness. Start with the available light and consider the available modes. Eventually, you may want to add a separate light source (such as a flash) and delve deeper into your camera's controls.

Finding the light

Exposure refers to the amount of light that enters the lens. You can think about light in several ways, such as the direction, intensity (brightness), color, and *quality* of light. To incorporate these characteristics of light into your compositions, here are a few tips:

✔ **Time of day:** The best light for photographs is usually around dawn or dusk. The light is warmer and softer, and the shadows are longer and less harsh. Avoid midday light when the sun causes harsh or sharp shadows and squinting. If you must shoot at noon, move your subject into shady areas or turn your flash on to reduce shadows on faces. (This is called a *fill flash* or *forced flash.*)

 The Flash control usually looks like a lightning bolt or spark. Press it repeatedly to cycle through options, including on or off. This may not be possible, if the camera keeps control of the flash in Auto mode.

✔ **Weather:** Cloudy or overcast days can be excellent for taking photos, especially portraits. The light is soft and diffused. An empty sky may be less interesting than one with clouds.

✔ **Direction:** Photographing a subject with *back-lighting* (lighting that comes from behind) can produce a dramatic image, as shown in

Figure 2-4. Avoid *lens flare* — nasty light circles or rainbow effects that mar images — by not having your brightest light source shine directly into your lens.

Photo credit: Mark Justice Hinton

Figure 2-4: Use backlighting creatively in an image.

Be careful shooting photos when the light source is directly behind your subject. Your camera may adjust the light meter to the lighter background and not to your subject, thereby creating an overly dark foreground or subject. If the exposure of the foreground subject is good, a bright background may be too bright in the photo. The effect can be dramatic or awful. Consider forcing the flash, if necessary.

Turn every rule or suggestion upside down to see for yourself whether it's valid. Have a shoot-out at high noon. Where some see ugly shadows, you may capture something strong or dramatic. (Remember, no one has to see your mistakes.)

✔ **Color:** The light at midday is white, the light at sunrise and sunset is orange and feels warm, and the light in shaded areas and at twilight is blue and appears cool.

Your camera's modes may push color in different directions in an effort to enhance the image.

Your camera's setup menu may offer color options such as vivid (to saturate color), sepia (to drain color), or black and white. I recommend the vivid option, unless it proves too lush for your tastes.

✔ **Creative:** When possible, use lighting creatively to lead the eye, create a mood, or evoke an emotion. Look for compositions created with light illuminating or shadowing an object.

Using contrast

Contrast describes the degree of difference between light and dark areas. High contrast defines stark differences between light and dark areas; low contrast appears softer and more muted.

Mixing light with dark provides contrast, which in turns creates impact, as shown in Figure 2-5.

Photo credit: Mark Justice Hinton

Figure 2-5: Contrasting light and dark creates impact and depth.

In color images, you can also achieve contrast by using complementary colors, such as red and green, yellow and blue, and cyan and orange. Look for contrast in both nature and your own setups.

Even basic photo editors enable changes to brightness and contrast after the fact.

Taking Some Fun Shots

Without delving any deeper into your camera's controls or photography's bigger picture (sorry, couldn't resist the pun), you can easily move beyond the standard snapshot. (Although snapshots have their place, and not every picture needs to be art.)

You should look into (they're coming frequently now) changing your perspective. Get closer to a tiny subject with your macro setting. Bring a distant subject closer to you with zoom. Squat, crouch, stretch to put the lens higher or lower than standing height.

Shooting close-ups in Macro mode

How close can you put your lens to an object and still take a clear photo? If you're too close, the photo may be blurry. For extreme close-ups, many cameras have a separate Macro mode to enable you to photograph objects within inches — even less than an inch, for some. Look for a flower symbol on the camera body and on-screen.

 Your camera may automatically switch in and out of Macro mode based on distance to the subject. Otherwise, use the Macro control.

A macro exposure makes the small large — even huge. Figure 2-6 shows a close-up of a one-inch June bug on a chamisa bush. The original scene is barely two inches square, but it fills a computer monitor larger than life.

You may need to experiment with exposure settings. Start with Automatic or the Sports setting (for things that move fast, such as bugs or flowers in a breeze).

 Don't use a flash with macros. A flash won't do any good that close and may ruin the shot. If your flash is set to Auto, you may have to suppress it (turn it off).

Figure 2-6: Set your camera to Macro mode for close-up shots.

For flowers and small creatures, you may want to get on your knees or stomach for a good shot. A movable LCD can spare you that effort by flipping up or out.

The closer you get to the subject, the greater the odds that you'll actually bump into it or cast a shadow over the subject. Even a breath of air can move the subject and cause blurring. Consider placing the camera on the ground or a tripod and using the self-timer.

Check your camera's documentation to find out the particular focusing distance that Macro mode is capable of. Less than an inch should be possible.

Follow these steps to take a macro exposure:

1. **Set the Mode dial or button to Macro on your camera.**

   Look for a flower icon.

2. **Compose your shot in the viewfinder or LCD screen.**

3. **Press the shutter button halfway to give your camera a moment to establish the shot.**

   Focusing in Macro mode can be tricky, so be sure that the subject you want is in focus; if it isn't, make the necessary adjustments.

4. **Press the shutter button the rest of way to capture the image.**

Shooting from unexpected angles

To see the world differently, change the way you look at it. Get down (or up). Walk around your subject, if you can, crouching and stretching. Try not to frighten people in the process.

Take some photos from angles other than straight on at five to six feet off the ground — the world of the average snapshot. Changing your viewpoint can exaggerate the size of the subject either larger or smaller, enhance the mood of the shot, or make a dull shot more interesting, as shown in Figure 2-7.

Depending on your particular subject, try a bird's-eye view (above the subject) or a worm's-eye view (below it).

Most flower photos are face on and nice enough. Try photographing flowers from the side or the back in the morning or evening — people seldom see this perspective.

Photo credit: Mark Justice Hinton

Figure 2-7: Use an unexpected angle to exaggerate a subject. (Don't push the red button!)

Zooming in on your subject

Whereas a macro shot gets you closer to something that's already close by, a telephoto shot brings the distant object close to you. Strictly speaking, a *telephoto* lens has a fixed focal length. A *zoom* lens is a magical lens that easily ranges from normal to telephoto and steps in between. On your camera, look for a long switch labeled *W* (for wide angle — normal) at one end and *T* (telephoto) at the other. This kind of switch is called a *rocker*.

Gently press the *T* end of this odd switch while looking through the viewfinder or LCD. Zoom. With your eye glued to the camera, press the *W* end. Zoom back. An electronic viewfinder or LCD may display the degree of zoom or magnification from 1x (normal) to the maximum for your camera (10x is 10 times closer than normal; 30x is the current maximum for non-DSLRs).

The scene in Figure 2-8 took place nearly half a mile from where I was sitting, along the Continental Divide Trail. The 20x zoom got me close enough. However, if I wanted closer pictures of the horses, I would have needed an even longer zoom.

Photo credit: Mark Justice Hinton

Figure 2-8: Zoom in to get closer to a distant subject.

Follow these steps to zoom:

1. **Choose a subject more than a few feet away. Press the T end of the Zoom rocker just enough to zoom closer to the subject.**

Zooming may be jerky or noisy on some cameras. You may not be able to zoom precisely to a particular point — over-zooming and under-zooming are common problems.

2. **Zoom in on your subject as close as you can get.**

3. **Press the W end of the rocker to zoom back out a little at a time.**

4. **Repeat this process with subjects that are close and others very far away.**

5. **Take as many photos as you like.**

   Get a sense of just how close you can get to a distant subject without moving toward it. (In practice, you may want to move closer and zoom in.)

You can use your zoom with subjects close by. Keep in mind that zooming in with an optical zoom shortens the depth of field (DOF). (Part III discusses DOF in depth. Ahem.) Objects outside the DOF — nearer or farther — will be out of focus; the background may become blurrier, as shown in the close-up of a coreopsis flower in front of a green lawn in Figure 2-9.

 An *optical* lens uses the optics of the camera (the lens) to bring the subject closer. A *digital* zoom isn't actually a zoom lens. It simply enlarges the center of the scene in the camera and crops out the rest. A digital zoom can degrade image resolution and quality. Therefore, you probably want to avoid using a digital zoom. If your camera has a digital zoom, you may have to disable the digital zoom by using a menu option. Some cameras switch to digital zoom if you zoom past the maximum optical setting. You may see an indication of the zoom level on the screen.

Photo credit: Mark Justice Hinton

Figure 2-9: You can zoom in on an object close by for special effect.

Some cameras enable you to use zoom and macro together. That may seem contradictory, but the result is a macro shot of a distant subject (refer to Figure 2-9). However, some cameras can't use these two together. If that's the case with your camera, make sure the Zoom rocker is all the way to the wide end before taking a macro shot. Check your owner's manual or experiment.

There are two ways to fill a frame with your subject. One is to zoom in from a distance until it fills the frame. Another is to get as close as possible, using Macro mode, if necessary. You should try taking the same picture both ways to get a better feel for the impact of your choice on exposure, background, and focus.

Reviewing Photos and Videos on Your Camera

You may want to see — and show — the pictures you've taken while they're still in your camera. That's instant gratification. Last century, people mailed film to a lab and waited weeks for their photos to come back on shiny bits of paper! A common reaction then was, "Why did I take that?"

In the new century, we no longer have to wait to see our photos and videos. You can see any or all of the photos on your card at any time. I don't know why this function is called *preview* — aren't you reviewing your photos? Look for a Preview button on the camera, which often shows a triangle pointing to the right and which may have green on the button.

If your camera has both an electronic viewfinder (EVF) and an LCD, you can see your photos on either. The LCD will be better, of course, but remember that your batteries are draining, in either case.

Some cameras automatically show the most recent picture you took for a few seconds. You may be able to turn that feature on or off in the setup menus. (This brief display can be distracting if you quickly shoot several pictures in a row.)

Review — I mean preview — your photos and videos with these steps:

1. **Press the Preview button.**

   If you don't see anything on the LCD, you may have to press the button that switches display between the LCD and the EVF. The picture you took most recently appears on-screen.

2. **To see other photos, press the left button to go backward or the right button to go forward through the photos (see Figure 2-10).**

   These buttons are usually at 3 o'clock (right) and 9 o'clock (left) on the buttons arranged in a circle.

Press to zoom in.

Press for more thumbnails.

Move through photos. See one photo.

See one or more photos.

Figure 2-10: Choose a thumbnail and press OK to see just that photo.

3. **Zoom into a picture by pressing the Zoom rocker toward telephoto (T). Press OK/Enter (the center of the circle of buttons) to return to normal display.**

   Zoomed in, the up, down, right, and left buttons usually move the zoomed-in area around the screen.

   You may be able to zoom out to display more than one photo at once as *thumbnails* (small versions). This display is called the *index*. Zoom out again to show more and smaller thumbnails, if possible. The up, down, right, and left buttons move the selection from one thumbnail to the next. Press OK/Enter to see the selected photo.

4. **To end Preview mode, press the Preview button a second time, switch modes, or turn off the camera.**

 Don't bother to delete or edit photos on the camera. Move them to your computer, instead.

Some cameras can connect to TVs using standard RCA, USB, or HDMI cables, allowing you to run a slide show on the TV. You use your camera or card to show your pictures on TV or a digital photo frame. You probably don't want to show every picture on your memory card, though.

Part III

Composing Better Shots

· ·

In This Part

▶ Bringing your images into focus

▶ Understanding depth of field

▶ Determining your focal point

▶ Boning up on the Rule of Thirds

▶ Finding balance in your photos

· ·

*O*ne of the great things about digital photography is that it doesn't require a lot of thought. You can simply point your camera and click the shutter. (Okay, you do have to remember to turn it on and remove the lens cap, if the camera doesn't do that automagically.)

A camera is like a computer. Wait, that's a good thing! A camera has capabilities that you can ignore as long as you like. When you start looking deeper, you find more and more that you can do with your camera.

Even if you're using the simplest point-and-shoot camera without any extra options, you still control the shot. You select the subject and frame it within your viewfinder.

In this Part, you look through the lens to see something new. You also explore various ideas for composing a photo to maximize your subject and minimize distractions.

Seeing through the Lens

Focus is vital in photography. A picture in focus is sharp and clear. A picture with the subject out-of-focus is probably a dud.

One problem with focusing a camera is that you're focusing your eye on something right in front of your face (the EVF or LCD), whereas your camera is focusing on the subject (you hope). Putting a lens (and everything else) between your eye and the subject requires seeing things in a slightly different way. It may help to understand how cameras focus and what you can do to control that.

Nailing your focus

When you raise your eyes from this page to look across the room, you continuously focus on whatever you're looking at. You don't think about fixing focus, unless you just woke up.

Most cameras don't work the way your eyes do, unless you change an option in setup. You can think of camera focus as consisting of three parts: when to focus, where in the frame to focus, and the distance between you and the subject. Each of these three elements can be handled by the camera or by you through your camera's setup menu or other controls.

When to focus

Normally, your camera only focuses when you press the shutter button halfway. That's why you do that, to give the camera a moment to focus (as well as to set exposure). That standard method of automatic focus (Auto Focus, or AF) is fine for subjects that aren't moving much. You simply need to get used to the fraction of a second delay as the camera focuses. (DSLRs don't usually have this focus delay. Refer to Part I for more about the different types of cameras.) Your camera may call this One Shot AF or Single Shot AF.

For subjects that are moving, you may need another form of automatic focus: Continuous Auto Focus (CAF). If CAF is available, it appears in a setup menu or as you press the Focus button, if your camera has one. As the name implies, CAF constantly focuses, even when you are not pressing the shutter button. An advantage of CAF is the elimination of that brief delay for focusing, which is great for catching subjects in motion. A disadvantage of CAF is the drain on the batteries caused by the constant focusing. CAF may also have some associated noise as it constantly adjusts focus, and this may result in a modest increase in wear and tear on the mechanism.

Cameras with a Sport mode (often a runner or soccer player icon) may use CAF automatically.

Where in the frame to focus

But what is the camera actually focusing on? Does a camera recognize the subject of a photo? You may want to focus on that pretty bird in the tree, while the camera is automatically focusing on the twig in the foreground, blurring the bird. What determines the *focal point* (the part of the frame used to focus)? Focal point sounds too small — think of this instead as the *focus area* that the camera uses to focus.

Your camera doesn't know what the subject of the photo is. Instead, your camera is set to focus on one or more areas within the frame. Standard AF uses a relatively wide area around the center of the frame to focus. You may see this as a rectangle or brackets on your EVF or LCD. (The rectangle or brackets may turn green when the subject is in focus.)

Your camera may let you choose Center Focus (CF).
With CF, the focus area is reduced to more of a
square than a broad rectangle. Use CF to reduce the
area the camera focuses on, such as when you want
to photograph one person in a crowd.

Some cameras feature Multipoint Focus (MF), in
which the camera focuses on a number of areas
(determined by the manufacturer, in most cases).

Some recent cameras have a variation on MF called
face detection, as well as *smile detection.* These cameras are programmed to recognize faces and smiles.
(Really!) Face detection draws a box around recognized faces, which the camera focuses on (among
other areas, in most cases). With smile detection, the
camera delays the shot until the subject smiles. Look
for a smiley face icon on your camera's controls.

Hats, sunglasses, or odd angles may confuse
face detection. Sometimes you'll see the face
detection box around something that's not a
face but has a pattern that fools the camera.
(Don't worry about that unless you don't want
the nonface in focus.)

The distance between you and the subject

Regardless of when or where the camera is focusing,
how does it know that your subject is 6 feet and not
20 feet away? This is another task that the brain handles subconsciously, in most cases, but cameras are
programmed to calculate.

Some cameras measure distance by using some form
of range-finder based on optics, infrared (especially in
low light), or sound (like a bat). This method is called
active autofocus. Lasers were used until the first few
subjects vanished in a puff of smoke. (Just kidding!)

Other cameras rely on *passive autofocus* methods known as phase detection or contrast measurement. Whereas active autofocus measures the distance to the subject, passive autofocus calculates the distance using analysis of light intensity differences at points on a sensor. The technical features of each method may be interesting, but for purposes of this Part, any form of autofocus works.

The camera's calculation or measurement of how far away the subject is can be affected by low light or objects between the lens and the subject. So, that's where Manual Focus comes in. Look for a Focus button or menu item on your camera to switch between Auto Focus and Manual Focus. When you choose Manual Focus, you tell your camera how far away the subject is by using left (closer) and right (farther) controls while watching a scale on-screen with distances marked up to infinity. Some cameras and lenses use a focus ring around the lens, instead. Manual Focus takes the control away from the camera and leaves it to you to guess distances accurately.

Locking focus

Most of the time, the camera automatically focuses on as many things in the frame as it can, but it may not include your subject or you may not want irrelevant objects in focus. Look for indications on-screen of where the camera is focusing (usually one or more boxes or brackets). If you want to force the camera to focus on a particular object, you can lock the focus on that object.

In most cases, pressing the shutter button halfway locks the focus until you press all the way down or release the button, no matter how focus was determined by the camera. You might deliberately lock focus on a subject before moving the camera a little to one side or the other. This takes the subject out of the center of the frame but ensures that the subject is in focus. An off-center subject may be more interesting, as long as the subject is in focus.

Be certain you don't change the distance between you and the object you lock focus on, by moving more than a small turn of your body or by zooming in or out. Moving more than side-to-side guarantees the subject will be out of focus.

You don't have to change any settings to try this technique. If you also want to prevent the camera from focusing on other objects in the frame, set the Auto Focus option to Center Focus mode. If your camera has an option to select a single focus point, select it. (Check your camera's user manual to find out how.)

Figure 3-1 shows an off-center subject. For this photo, I pressed the shutter button halfway down to lock the focus with the subject in the center of the frame. Then I moved the camera to create a more interesting composition.

Locking focus on a subject can help you in situations where the camera might focus on the wrong thing. For example, when you're photographing a bird in a tree, the camera might focus on branches closer to you than the bird. To adjust for this, focus on an object the same distance from you as the bird, lock the focus, and move the camera to frame the bird. (This trick works on other subjects, too. It requires a good sense of distance, as does Manual Focus.)

Photo credit: Mark Justice Hinton

Figure 3-1: Lock the focus before you shoot an off-center subject.

Working with depth of field

No matter which mechanism your camera uses to focus — Auto Focus, Manual Focus, Center Focus, Multipoint Focus — there is always the issue of depth of field (DOF). There is a range in front of the focal point (the area between the camera and the subject) and beyond or behind the subject that is in focus — that's the DOF.

Imagine three rows of volleyball players standing on bleachers. If the camera focuses on the middle row, will the players in the first and last row be in focus? They will be if there is sufficient DOF. If the DOF is shallow, the other rows will be out of focus. That may be just what you want if you like someone in the middle row.

Aperture directly affects DOF. If you are operating in any mode other than Aperture Priority, Program mode, or Manual mode, the aperture setting remains in the camera's control, along with the DOF. There is nothing wrong with letting the camera manage settings. When you control the aperture and DOF settings, you may create photos that are different from what the camera would do automatically. Those photos may be better, but some surely will be worse as you experiment. You have to break a lot of eggs to photograph an omelet.

To play around with DOF, look in the early morning and late afternoon for natural spotlighting of bright objects in front of darker, shaded backgrounds.

Figure 3-2 shows an image of a coneflower with a very shallow depth of field, resulting in a blurred background (called *bokeh*).

Photo credit: Mark Justice Hinton

Figure 3-2: An image with a shallow depth of field.

Figure 3-3, on the other hand, shows Lily Pond in Colorado, with a very deep depth of field that results in near and far objects that look equally sharp.

Photo credit: Mark Justice Hinton

Figure 3-3: An image with a deep depth of field.

If you want to create a shallow depth of field, use one of the techniques from the following list:

  ✔ **Shoot in Portrait mode.** Look for an icon of head and shoulders. This mode sets the camera to a larger aperture.

✔ **Set your camera to Aperture Priority (A or Av) mode, if that option is available.** Choose a wide aperture, which, ironically, is indicated by a lower f-stop number. For example, f2.8 is a larger aperture than f16. Try various aperture settings to create the DOF you're looking for.

✔ **Zoom in to fill your frame with the subject.**
The longer the focal length of your lens, the
shallower the DOF.

✔ **Move close to your subject.** The closer you are,
the shallower the DOF. A Macro shot has very
little DOF.

 With most non-DSLR cameras, you won't really
see the DOF until you look at the picture after-
ward. DSLRs may have a Preview button that
helps you see the DOF.

In you want to create a deep DOF, try one of these
techniques:

✔ **Shoot in Landscape mode.** Look for the
mountain icon on your camera. This mode
sets the camera to a narrower aperture.

✔ **Set your camera to Aperture Priority (A or Av)
mode.** Choose a narrower aperture (larger
number), such as f16 or f22. Experiment with
settings to create the depth of field you want.

✔ **Use a wide-angle lens (or less zoom, unless the
subject is very far away).** This increases the
impact of a deep DOF.

✔ **Move farther away from your subject.** The farther away a subject is, the greater the DOF.

 Keep in mind that DOF refers to how much area
is *in focus* in front and in back of your subject.
When you want to minimize a busy, distracting
background and make your subject a strong
focal point, use a shallow DOF, which blurs the
background. When you want the entire image
(from the foreground to the background) to be
sharply in focus, use a deep DOF.

Compact P&S cameras inherently have greater DOF due to their small sensors and short lenses. That makes it harder to reduce DOF. Use the zoom and move close to your subject (fill the frame). You may achieve the desired effect, especially if there is some distance between the subject and the background.

Composing the Photograph

So far, I've had you pretty fixated on technology — simply nailing down how to find and select the right setting for a particular shot. In this section, I help you snap up some technique (okay, bad pun). People have been taking and viewing photographs for ages, and you get to benefit from all they've learned.

The concept of *point-and-shoot* belies the amount of thought that precedes good *composition,* which is the conscious arrangement of elements in a scene. Along with juggling various mechanical settings — or using Automatic mode — consider improving the composition of your photograph by incorporating the suggestions discussed in this section. You find out how to place and enhance the subject, how to minimize distractions, and some ways to develop a particular mood for a shot. You may also see some photos that defy guidelines but are interesting, nonetheless.

Choosing your orientation

Most of the time, people hold a camera horizontally, the way it hangs from a strap or sits on a table. This is referred to as *landscape orientation.* The resulting photos will be wider than they are tall.

You may choose to rotate the camera 90 degrees left or right, holding the camera vertically. This is *portrait orientation.* The resulting photos will be taller than they are wide.

It may seem obvious from the names that landscape is suitable for pictures of, well, landscapes, and portrait orientation for pictures of people. Okay — it *is* obvious. Nevertheless, choosing the orientation of the camera is your first decision about composition. The orientation determines the emphasis of the picture — width, height, or depth — as well as the location of the thirds you are considering as you shoot.

Which perspective suits the subject? You might think portrait suits a person, but what if the scene around her is important? Consider landscape in that case. (Take shots in each orientation.) You'd have to think landscape orientation for a landscape scene, but what if you want to lead the eye up a valley or along a ridge you're standing on? Try portrait to emphasize the depth or length. (Take both.)

 One of the simplest edits is to *crop* a picture, which means that you save the part you want and throw the rest away. Cropped photos can be square or use other proportions than those of a standard print.

Figure 3-4 shows two photographs of the same subject in different orientations.

You will probably use landscape orientation more often than portrait. However, experiment with portrait (vertical) landscapes and landscape (horizontal) portraits. Shoot the same photo both ways. Uncommon orientation can add freshness to a subject.

Photo credit: Mark Justice Hinton

Figure 3-4: Landscape (top) or portrait (bottom) orientation is your first composition decision.

For portrait orientation, I hold the camera with the grip at the top. It's easier to let the camera's weight hang than to hold it with the grip at the bottom.

You're going to look at your photos on a screen, whether computer, TV, or photo frame. Screens are usually landscape. Portrait-oriented photos will have big, black borders on the left and right. Objects in the photo will be smaller than in a similar landscape shot because the height of the photo is reduced to fit the wider screen. In the worst case, some devices stretch the photo left and right, resulting in the top and bottom disappearing off-screen.

Finding a focal point

If a photo contains too many elements, the eye doesn't know where to look first. Beware the wandering eye. A focal point draws your viewer to a main point of interest within the image. One of the easiest compositional tasks is to find a clearly defined focal point.

Consider a city street corner with a lot of traffic signs, a couple of billboards, and dozens of people moving in every direction. That chaos might actually be the subject of a photo. But if the actual subject is a dog sitting by a lamppost, people looking at the photo may miss that point. (The *Where's Waldo?* series proves people enjoy hunting for the subject under some circumstances.)

A clear focal point should include only necessary elements that contribute to the compositional strength or emotional impact of your image, eliminating distractions. Here are a couple of suggestions:

✔ **Zoom in.** If you're photographing people or animals, try to get close to them by moving or using a zoom lens. (Using the zoom allows for more candid photos.)

✔ **Find an interesting subject.** If you're shooting outdoor scenes, give people something to focus on. Shots of mountains and beaches are fine, but how many are truly memorable? Throw in a climber scaling the mountain wall or a surfer wiping out on a wave and you elevate the visual impact to another level.

Elements that distract from your focal point, and which you should try to avoid, include too much background and random clutter and bystanders.

Figure 3-5 shows an off-center focal point (a sunflower seedling) emphasized by natural lighting.

Photo credit: Mark Justice Hinton

Figure 3-5: The focal point can be anywhere in the frame.

Every guideline has exceptions. A field of flowers may not have a focal point but smells as sweet.

Reducing background clutter

Most people worry only about cutting off people's heads when they shoot. (Now that's a gruesome sentence!) However, including too many elements in their shots distracts from the focal point. Try to eliminate background clutter that adds nothing to the value of your shot.

Here are a few tips for reducing unnecessary elements in your photo compositions:

✔ **Get close.** Fill your frame with your subject.

✔ **Move your camera, yourself, or your subject.** Try shooting a vertical or diagonal shot if the subject warrants it. If moving your camera isn't enough, move around your subject and try unexpected angles. Look for compositions that minimize or avoid distracting elements around your subject, such as poles, wires, fences, or bright lights.

✔ **Include only complementary background elements.** If your background elements are interesting and give context to your subject, include them. These elements can include props, landmarks, and natural components.

✔ **Try blurring an unavoidable, undesirable background.** Sometimes you can do this by using a wider aperture on your camera. This strategy makes the depth of field shallower so that your subject is sharp but the background isn't.

You can move around your subject, choosing the least distracting or most interesting background for your shot.

Following the Rule of Thirds

Very few photographic guidelines have been elevated to the status of a *rule,* but this section tells you about one of them. The Rule of Thirds divides the photo into horizontal thirds, vertical thirds, or a grid of nine squares (3 x 3).

For a very simple example of the effect of thirds, stand where you can see the horizon. Looking through the VF or using the LCD, position the horizon one-third up from the bottom of the frame. Shoot or take a mental picture. Move the camera slightly to position the horizon two-thirds up from the bottom. Which of these pictures is better depends on your intent and the subject. Either may be better than dividing the frame in half with the horizon.

Figure 3-6 shows a photo of a Canada goose overlaid with a grid. The Rule of Thirds suggests that the focal point should be at or near one of the four intersections around the middle of the picture, along one of the thirds — vertical, horizontal, or both. Placing the subject or focal point along the thirds makes it more likely to be noticed first and, some say, is subconsciously more pleasing.

Remember, the Rule of Thirds is only a guideline. A very strict use of thirds would shift the goose's body down to the next intersection, but that would wreck the reflection.

Photo credit: Mark Justice Hinton

Figure 3-6: Position your subject by using the Rule of Thirds.

Your camera may have an option to turn on gridlines. Some cameras don't show gridlines in Auto mode, but only in one of the manual modes.

To apply the Rule of Thirds to various shots, consider these examples:

✔ **In a scenic shot:** A low horizon creates a spacious feeling; a high horizon gives an intimate feeling.

✔ **In a portrait:** Try putting the face or eyes of the person along a vertical or horizontal third or at one of the four points of intersection.

If you have a camera with Auto Focus, lock the focus when you're moving from center because the Auto Focus sensor locks onto whatever is in the center of the viewfinder (unless you've manually chosen a different focus method). Center your subject in the viewfinder and apply slight pressure to the shutter release button to lock the focus. Then reposition your subject at an intersecting point and press the shutter release the rest of the way to take the photo.

Even the mighty Rule of Thirds has exceptions. You may choose to put your subject dead center, knowing that you expect to crop the picture later, either filling the frame with the subject or cropping with the subject off-center (and, more than likely, along one of the thirds).

Photography is fun. Editing is work.

Avoiding mergers

As you intently frame and compose your photo, you might fail to see a branch in the background that will seem to grow out of your friend's ear in the final photo. Such a gaffe is called a *merger.* Or, you might not notice that you're chopping off someone's hand or foot. This is known as a *border merger.*

Effects like these are common and amusing and, with luck, not too embarrassing. You can avoid mergers by thoroughly scanning the preview in the EVF or LCD and thinking about the background and foreground as much as you do about the subject. You may be able to avoid a problem with the background by moving your position or by reducing the depth of field (widening the aperture with a lower f-stop).

Figure 3-7 shows a border merger attacking a cheetah.

With the best photo-editing software and enough time, it's easier to brush away a branch than to restore a severed limb.

Photo credit: Corbis Digital Stock

Figure 3-7: Avoid border mergers.

Looking for balance

Even still photos can convey a sense of motion. A subject dead center may seem pinned or frozen in place. A subject along one of the thirds, looking or moving toward the center or away, creates tension between elements in the photo and the unseen world beyond the frame. You create balance in an image through the arrangement or placement of the elements in the image. Balance can be *symmetrical* (harmonious or formal) or *asymmetrical* (dynamic or informal). Think of balance in regard to color, shape, and contrast.

Imagine two photographs of a chessboard. In the first, all the pieces are lined up before the game begins. Shot from above or from the level of the board, the scene has a natural symmetry and balance among the pieces.

Now, the game is over. In a corner, two pieces stand over the fallen king — checkmate! The unbalanced image is part of the story.

The two photos in Figure 3-8 show very different approaches to the same subject (a church in Antigua, Guatemala) — starting with the orientation. The landscape photo on the top captures the symmetry and balance inherent in the architecture. The effect is formal and respectful. The portrait on the bottom intentionally unbalances the scene to draw the eye upward. The effect is more abstract and intimate.

Although the examples mentioned are not from nature, balance, motion, and symmetry all apply to any scene. Refer to Figure 3-6, in which the reflection in the water creates balance. The placement and direction of the goose suggest she is about to swim out of the scene.

Photo credit: Merri Rudd / Mark Justice Hinton

Figure 3-8: The symmetry and balance in a scene may convey formality or motion.

Finding leading lines

With some photos, your eye wanders haphazardly across the image, which isn't necessarily a bad thing. However, you may want to compose a stronger picture that leads the eye purposefully across the image.

Leading lines draw the eye into the picture. They add dimension and depth and can be actual lines or lines implied by the composition of elements.

To compose photos with leading lines, look for elements such as roads, fences, rivers, and bridges. Diagonal lines are dynamic. Curved lines are harmonious. Horizontal lines are peaceful. Vertical lines are active — or so some people say. Regardless of emotive quality, a line leads the eye.

The line of clouds in this photo of Chaco Canyon, New Mexico, shown in Figure 3-9, demonstrates how a leading line can direct your eye across an image. In Figure 3-9, the horizon (along the lower third) doesn't draw the eye left or right. The clouds lead the eye toward the lower right — and there's Waldo! This print may be too small for you to see the photographer's shadow in the lower-right corner. Such a shadow is generally regarded as a mistake. Here, it was intentional.

Photo credit: Mark Justice Hinton

Figure 3-9: Leading lines (the clouds, in this case) bring the eye into and across the image.

Keeping the horizon straight

For some reason, people expect horizons to be horizontal. (That must have something to do with the real world.) You can spoil a dramatic sunrise or sunset by too much tilt to the left or right. Try to keep a straight head on your shoulders or learn to compensate for your natural inclinations.

Figure 3-10 shows a whimsical self-portrait. The nearest horizontal line is perfectly level (and along one third, as is the foot). The real horizon is nearly along one third. Does it matter that it's not perfectly horizontal? If it were, then the shoreline wouldn't be. Sometimes, you have to make choices.

Photo credit: Merri Rudd

Figure 3-10: Keep major lines straight, when possible.

If your camera has a viewfinder screen with a built-in grid for the purpose of helping you keep the horizon straight, use it.

Using a tripod can also help keep your horizons straight. And some tripods come with built-in bubble levels. Just make sure that the legs of your tripod are extended properly — equally on level ground, or lopsidedly on uneven ground — to make the camera level.

Once you know the rules, you can always break them. But it's much more fun to break the rules you know than to operate out of ignorance.

Framing the subject

The term *frame* is used to describe the image itself. You frame your subject, and the lines in the composition, such as the horizon or roads — as well as movement — extend beyond the frame. Inside this frame, you can further frame the subject by including elements around the foreground that surround the subject. Imagine a lake appearing flanked by trees or a shot through a doorway or window looking inside or looking outside.

Figure 3-11 shows a doorway in Chaco Canyon framing part of a room beyond within the frame of the photo. The doorway in this photo may violate the Rule of Thirds because the right edge cuts the scene in half, unless you imagine the left-hand vertical third down the middle of the doorway. Showing more of the wall to the right would be more in line with the Rule of Thirds (one-third doorway, two-thirds wall).

Here are a few more points to keep in mind about framing within a photo:

- ✓ **A frame welcomes you to an image, adds depth, and creates a point of reference.**

- ✓ **To compose photos with frames, use foreground elements to frame your subjects.** Elements such as tree branches, windows, and doorways can frame wide or long shots. Close-up shots can also be framed.

- ✓ **Decide whether to keep your framing elements sharply focused or soft.** Depending on the shot, sometimes sharply focused framing elements can distract from, rather than enhance, the focal point.

Photo credit: Mark Justice Hinton

Figure 3-11: It can be fun to put frames within frames.

Creating a mood with distance

A memorable photograph often creates or conveys a mood. The subject is clearly significant, but light and distance also impart a mood.

Getting close to your subject may make the image personal, warm, and inviting. Avoid including excessive background elements, and intimately fill your frame with your subject, especially when photographing people.

Figure 3-12 shows the subject's joy in an odd find on the trail (a gastrolith). This photo illustrates the intimacy that comes with getting close to your subject.

Photo credit: Mark Justice Hinton

Figure 3-12: Getting close to your subject affects the mood of the picture.

You might even violate guidelines for framing and against mergers by getting exaggeratedly close to your subject. A close-up of a face, even just eyes, nose, and mouth, can be very interesting. A good zoom lens allows you to get especially close without aggravating your subject.

And just as shooting close can create a feeling of intimacy, shooting a subject with a lot of space around it can evoke a sense of loneliness or isolation (refer to Figure 3-9). It all depends on your intended message.

 Use eye contact when photographing people. Remember that children, animals, and other height-challenged subjects aren't at the same eye level as adults. Try getting down on the ground, to their level, if necessary.

Using texture and shape

When composing your shot, look for interesting textures to add definition and for lines and shapes to create interest. Remember that textures and shapes are enhanced by the use of light and shadow. These elements come into play even more when you're shooting black-and-white images.

Figure 3-13 shows the effect of texture in an image. This photo of a rock wall in Chetro Ketl, New Mexico, emphasizes the natural texture of the stone plus the sculptural quality of the mason's work. This photo might be even more interesting in black and white.

 Check your camera's settings or refer to your user's guide to see whether your camera offers a black-and-white (B&W) setting. Alternatively, you can switch from color to B&W during editing.

Photo credit: Mark Justice Hinton

Figure 3-13: Using texture for added definition.

Part IV

Transferring Photos from Camera to Computer

*E*ventually, you'll want to transfer the photos from your camera to your computer so that you can edit, share, print, or simply store them. (And, it's definitely preferable to throwing the camera away because it's full.)

After you move the pictures to your computer, you can free up space on the camera for more photos . . . and the vicious cycle begins. That cycle never really ends, and it can eat up more and more of your computer's hard drive space. Photo files are typically megabytes in size. A few hundred photos can add up to a gigabyte of disk space in no time. Consider investing in an external hard drive that is larger than you can imagine using. Disk space, like closets and garages, seem to fill up when you aren't looking. An external hard drive is much more convenient than storing photos on DVDs or CDs, but you do have to think about creating a second copy — a backup — no matter where you store your photos.

With photos on your computer, you can enjoy all the effort you've made taking those pictures. The photos on your computer are instantly available for viewing individually, as slide shows, and as screen savers.

In this Part, I show you how to transfer your photos from your camera to your hard drive. After those photos are on the hard drive, you'll surely need to copy, move, delete, and rename those files. I show you how to do all this with Windows 7 Explorer; other operating systems work similarly.

Deleting Photos from Your Camera Manually

Despite your blossoming photographic skill, you'll eventually take some pictures that just aren't worth keeping. You can delete pictures directly from your camera's memory card to free up space for newer pictures. To delete photos directly from the camera, you don't need a computer or a cable.

Before I show you how to delete photos from your camera, let me make one suggestion: Don't do it! It's just too easy to delete the wrong picture. And you can't judge a picture completely on the tiny LCD. You need to see it on your large computer monitor. Perhaps the picture has details worth cropping. Perhaps you can improve the picture with other edits (make it lighter or darker, among other possibilities).

Get a memory card large enough to hold all the pictures you might take before you have a chance to move them to the computer. See Part I for more about memory cards and photo file sizes.

Now, just so you know how, because knowledge is a beautiful thing, here are the steps for deleting photos from the camera memory card. Take a couple of bad photos before you continue:

1. **Using the camera's LCD, switch to Preview mode.**

   Look for a button that shows a right-pointing triangle.

2. **In Preview mode, use the right- and left-arrow buttons to move through a display of your pictures.**

   You may be able to press the W (Wide) end of the Zoom rocker switch to see multiple photos at once.

3. **When you find a photo you don't want to keep, press your camera's Delete button (look for a trash can icon) or a Delete menu item on-screen, as shown in Figure 4-1.**

   Some cameras require confirmation of the delete instruction. Press OK if needed.

That wasn't so hard. Why the fuss? Many people delete a photo thinking they'll take a better one later — but they never do. Even a bad picture might be better than no picture at all. So transfer that photo to your computer, review it there, and think twice before dumping it.

Figure 4-1: Your camera may have a Delete button or menu item.

 To get rid of every photo on the camera in one step — are you sure you want to do this? — use the camera's setup menu to format or erase the memory card. There is no Undo for formatting or erasing a memory card. So be very sure that this is what you want to do. Again, *you can't undo this!*

Planning Before You Copy Photos

Before you copy any photos to your computer, think about how you want to organize those files. Even if you're using a tool that automatically copies photos, you have to configure that tool to serve your sense of order.

It's important to recognize that your organizational style is unique and also likely to change over time. When you can't find that one picture you want most, you may have to let it go. But learn from that search as you copy more and more pictures to your computer, and continue to refine your photo organization. Consider what changes to your system will make it easier to find pictures the next time.

How you name the photo files and the folders they go into is very important for organizing and reorganizing photos. Think about whether you should include some descriptive text in the filename, such as *vacation* or *Colorado vacation*. And is it helpful to include some part of the date in the file or folder name?

An option called a *tag* offers a way for you to add descriptive categories to your photos, providing further means of organizing your files so that you can easily find them later with a simple search for specific tags.

Naming files

Your camera names each photo file as it creates it. That name usually includes a sequential or random number or the date and time. Your camera's setup menu may allow you to select the method used to name files. Options for naming files on the camera may include specifying whether the number in each filename is continuous, meaning it never resets. If that option is enabled, every file has a unique filename. If that option is disabled, numbering starts over with each new set of photos, resulting in duplicate filenames. This point may be irrelevant if you rename files as you copy them, but many professional photographers keep these camera-generated filenames and want them to be unique.

Filenames also include a three-letter file *extension* — the three additional letters that follow the period (.) in a filename. The extension is determined by the file format you select in the camera's setup menus. Most likely, your files are JPEGs with the file extension .jpg. If your camera creates files in the RAW format, the extension name depends on the camera.

If you use an automatic process to copy your photos from camera to disk, that process may rename those files according to options set within that program.

Which is a better filename: DSC0047.jpg or vacation.jpg? *Vacation* may seem to be the better choice if you take only one vacation and save only one photo from that trip. But think through the kind of overall file-naming scheme that might work best for you.

Figure 4-2 shows some photos as extra-large thumbnail images (or icons) on the right and folders on the left in Windows Explorer in Windows 7. The gap in the sequence of filenames under each photo is due to deletions. (*Note:* The extension name (.jpg) is normally hidden in Windows.) The folder *path* appears at the top of the screen.

Libraries ▶ Pictures ▶ My Pictures

Using folders

How you name your individual photos is important, but you also want folders to hold specific photo files in an organized, logical way for easy access in the future.

The best way to organize groups of files is to create folders in which to store them. Some people also create folders within folders (called *subfolders*).

Although you can create folders anytime, it is easiest to create folders during the process of copying photos from camera to disk.

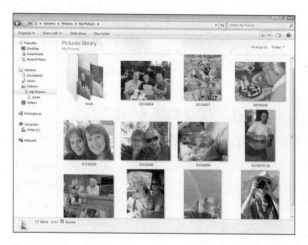

Figure 4-2: The sequential, camera-generated filenames matter less in this organizational style than folders and tags.

A folder's name should help you recognize its contents as you shuffle madly through, looking for the vacation photos from three — or was it four? — years ago.

For example, you could have the following series of folders within folders:

```
Pictures
   2010
       Vacations
           South Pacific
           Hawaii
```

Or maybe this simpler structure makes more sense:

```
Pictures
   Hawaii
```

As you name folders, keep in mind how your computer displays folders: Generally, folders are sorted either by name or by the date modified, although other options are available.

Getting Pictures Out of Your Camera

Most cameras can connect directly to a computer by using a USB cable and the ports on the camera and the computer. The port on your camera could be just about anywhere on the camera body, and it may be hidden by a small door or cover. Plug one end of the cable into the camera and the other end into the USB port on your computer (see Figure 4-3). Turn the camera power on, if necessary.

In most cases, the computer automatically recognizes the camera and begins copying photos from the camera to the computer.

If your computer doesn't recognize the camera and nothing happens automatically, you may need to install a *driver,* a program that tells the computer how to talk to hardware. Odds are that using a driver won't be necessary, though. If manually installing a driver does turn out to be necessary, you may find that a CD containing the driver software that came with your camera. Instead of using that CD, go to the camera manufacturer's Web site and download and install the latest driver for your specific camera model and your specific computer operating system

(Windows, Macintosh, or Linux). (Again, this process probably happens automatically.)

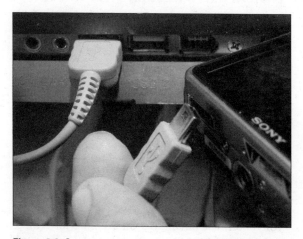

Figure 4-3: Connect camera and computer with a cable.

 When you travel, take the USB cable so that you can transfer photos from your camera to your laptop or a friend's computer.

Instead of plugging your camera into the computer, you can insert your camera memory card into a *card reader*. Many laptops have a built-in card reader slot that takes various card types, such as SD. If your computer doesn't have a built-in card reader, you can buy a separate device that plugs into your computer. Another option is to buy an adapter designed to convert a memory card into a flash drive. You remove the memory card from the camera and insert it into the card reader (or converter). Just like when you connect the camera directly, inserting a memory card in a card reader should start the copying process automatically.

Copying photos from your camera automatically

In most cases, connecting a camera to a computer automatically starts the copying of pictures from the camera to the computer.

 Your camera may come with software for moving, organizing, and editing your pictures. Before you install more software, see what happens without that software. You may already have everything you need for basic tasks.

With the pictures safely on your computer, you can delete them from the camera without regret. In fact, the automatic copying process probably includes an option to automatically delete all pictures on the camera after the copying completes successfully. Take advantage of that automatic delete — it will save you time. If you intend to print from the card (directly to a printer or at a print service) or to use the card in a digital photo frame, then don't automatically delete photos from the card.

The following steps show you how to use the Import Pictures and Videos function in Windows 7 to transfer photos from your camera to your computer.

1. **Connect your camera or card reader to your computer by using a USB cable.**

   Alternatively, if your computer has a media card slot or you have a card reader, insert your card.

   The AutoPlay dialog box appears, as shown in Figure 4-4.

2. **Select the Import Pictures and Videos Using Windows option to import your images.**

   You may see additional import options if you have a photo organizer installed.

To use the Open Folder to View Files function, see the next section, "Copying Photos from Your Camera Manually."

Figure 4-4: Windows may give you a choice of how to copy your photos.

If you have any photo management software installed, such as Windows Live Photo Gallery, that software may pop up instead of the AutoPlay options. Just click Cancel or exit that program for the purposes of these steps. If you prefer to use that software, follow that program's documentation for transferring your photos.

The Import Pictures and Videos dialog box appears (see Figure 4-5).

   3. **(Optional) Add a tag for the photos.**

   4. **Click the Import button.**

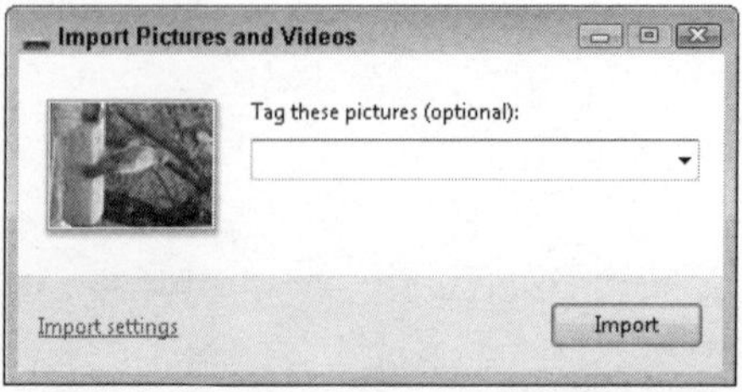

Figure 4-5: The Import Pictures and Videos dialog box in Windows 7.

    The dialog box displays a progress bar and the count of photos being copied.

   5. **Click the Erase after Importing check box to automatically delete the photos from the camera (recommended).**

    Some people prefer to format the card in camera after the transfer.

    After the copying and erasing are done, Explorer opens automatically to a window like the one in Figure 4-6. The filenames (001, 002, and so forth) were determined by the import settings.

Figure 4-6: Recently imported photos.

Copying photos from your camera manually

Ideally, when you plug your camera into your computer with a USB cable, your computer automatically copies your pictures from the camera to your computer's hard drive. However, when your camera is attached to your computer, the camera's memory card is listed as a removable disk in Computer (or My Computer if you're using XP). You can browse that disk as you can any other, working your way into the folders to find the individual photo files. From there, you can copy, move, and delete files.

Avoid renaming files still on the camera because renaming them may interfere with the camera's automatic naming function.

The following steps show you how to use Windows Explorer in Windows 7 to transfer photos from your camera to your computer:

1. **Connect your camera to your computer by using a USB cable.**

   If your computer has a media card slot or you have a card reader, insert your card. If your camera has a docking station, plug it into your computer and place your camera in the dock.

   The Windows AutoPlay dialog box opens (refer to Figure 4-4).

2. **Choose the Open Folder to View Files command to launch Windows Explorer.**

   If nothing happens automatically, launch Windows Explorer manually by choosing Start⇨ Computer.

3. **In Windows Explorer, select Computer to display all disks, including your camera or memory card. See Figure 4-7. Click or double-click the icon for the camera.**

4. **Select the camera folder containing your images.**

   If you see more than one folder, you may have to look in each one until you find your photos.

5. **Copy the photos you want.**

   Press Ctrl+A to select all the photos in the folder and then press Ctrl+C to copy.

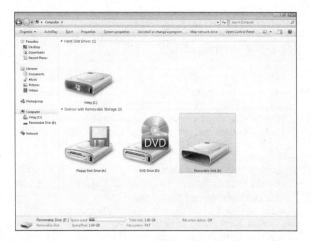

Figure 4-7: Your memory card is just another disk.

6. **In the navigation bar on the left, select Pictures or choose Start⇨Pictures.**

7. **Choose the folder where you want to save these photos:**

   • *An existing folder:* Open that folder.

   • *A new folder:* Click the New Folder button in the Explorer Command bar or choose Organize⇨New Folder. Type a name for your new folder and press Enter. Open the new folder.

8. **Press Ctrl+V to paste the photos into the folder.**

   Filenames remain the same as they are on the camera unless you manually rename the files.

Viewing Photos on Your Computer

When you have photos on your computer, you can view them and begin to work with them in various ways. In this section, I show you how Windows 7 handles photos. However, you may have a program installed that takes over these duties from Windows 7, such as Windows Live Photo Gallery (WLPG).

Access your photo folder using Windows Explorer, the file manager in Windows 7. In Explorer, you can see your photos as thumbnails (or icons) of various sizes, as well as see some information about your photos. Explorer also enables you to copy, move, rename, and delete photos. (All of these tasks can also be performed using a photo organizing program, such as WLPG.)

You can explore your photos the following ways:

- **Choose a view:** Click the View button in the upper right of Explorer to change how you see your photos:

  - *Choose the size of the icons (thumbnails).* For best viewing, select Extra Large Icons from the list.

  - *Choose to see all the details:* Details lists files in rows and information such as filename, date, and size in columns.

- **Arrange your photos by date:** Click the button next to Arrange By and select Day from the list (see Figure 4-8). Your photos are arranged by date taken. Choose Arrange By⇨Folder if you wish to return to the original order.

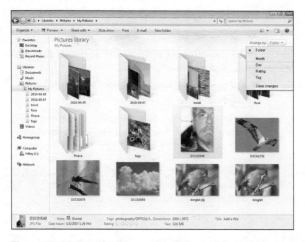

Figure 4-8: View and arrange your photos.

> ✔ **View a photo full screen:** Click the photo once
> to select it. In the Command bar, click the trian-
> gle next to Open for a list of programs with
> which you can open this photo. Windows Photo
> Viewer is standard with Windows 7, as is Paint.
> If you want to open with the default photo pro-
> gram, you can double-click the photo or click
> the Open button, just not on the triangle.

For information on using Windows 7, see
Windows 7 For Dummies by Andy Rathbone or
Windows 7 For Seniors For Dummies, by Mark
Justice Hinton.

Renaming Photos

If you want to rename your photos (or any file) in
Windows Explorer, follow these steps:

1. **In Explorer, select the files.**

   To select all, press Ctrl+A.

2. **With the mouse pointer over the first file, right-click and choose Rename.**

3. **Type the new filename in the highlighted box and press Enter.**

   If you see an extension name following a period, do not change that part of the filename. You may not be able to open your photo if you do.

   Windows renames all the selected files using the name you type followed by a number in parentheses.

Backing Up Your Photos

You move your photos from your camera to your computer. Now all your eggs are in one basket. I doubt it's news to you that something could go wrong. You may delete or misedit the only copy you have of a beloved photo. That file may become corrupted and unusable. I'm not trying to scare you, but something could make your computer disappear. (Not any particular keystroke that I know of.)

The more important your photos are to you, the more you need duplicates — backups. You can back up your entire computer or just the pictures that matter. You can use the software that comes with your computer. Check the main system menu or search your computer for *backup*. Free alternatives also exist. Search the Web for *backup software review*.

A backup program has many benefits, including automatic scheduling (daily, weekly, and so on) or archiving (keeping multiple copies of the same file as it changes). Such backup features take time to understand and configure. That is time well spent, but beyond the scope of this book. You should include all your irreplaceable files in a good backup plan.

All photo editors, such as Windows Live Gallery, allow you to undo some edits before you save the file. Some editors enable you to revert to the original, even after saving. The safest thing is to create backups before you begin editing. Backing up may save you from all kinds of missteps, goofs, surprises, and disasters. The assurance of a backup will make you feel freer to experiment and learn.

Whether you intend to back up photos for peace of mind or simply to copy them to take them to another computer, follow these steps:

1. **Insert a flash drive (a thumb-sized device) into a USB port on your computer.**

   These steps also work with a memory card or external hard drive.

   If Windows automatically opens a list of available programs, close that window. If Windows starts some program, exit that program.

2. **Select the photos you intend to copy using Explorer.**

   One way to select multiple files individually is to hold down the Ctrl key as you select each file. To select all, press Ctrl+A.

3. **Right-click and choose Send To⇨*your device name*.**

   The device you inserted in Step 1 appears near the bottom of the list with a letter (D: or higher). See Figure 4-9.

Figure 4-9: Use the Send To function to copy photos to other disks.

The next time you want to copy photos, if you want to copy only those photos you haven't copied before (makes sense), arrange the photos by date taken. See the earlier section, "Viewing Photos on Your Computer," for the steps.

To copy photos to a DVD or CD, click the Burn button in the Command bar.

Deleting Photos from Your Computer

You will want to get rid of some photos on your computer.

If you find photos that must go, follow these steps:

1. **Select the photos you intend to delete.**
2. **Press the Delete key or right-click and choose Delete.**
3. **If a confirmation dialog box appears, click OK.**

If you change your mind immediately, press Ctrl+Z or right-click and choose Undo Delete.

If you want to restore a photo (or any file) you deleted, open the Recycle Bin from the desktop. Locate the file. Right-click and choose Restore.

Part V

Getting the Right Exposure

. . . .

In This Part

▶ Controlling the shutter speed

▶ Getting comfortable with aperture settings

▶ Being sensitive to ISO

. . . .

*L*ook off at a spot exactly four feet in front of your face. (Okay, look around first to make sure no one is watching.) How hard is that? Now, using your eyes — not your camera — make everything five feet away blurry. Can't do it? Cameras can do that: focus precisely and vary the depth of field (DOF) — really the depth of *focus,* with blurring nearer and farther than the DOF.

The point is, the lens isn't really just an extension of your eye. Cameras and eyes (plus brains) have very different optics and follow different rules. You don't have to master camera optics, but you need to be aware that certain factors can affect what you get out of your camera.

This Part can help you move out of the preset scene modes into various manual options. You start to juggle settings that the scene modes handle automatically for you. DSLRs have many different settings. High-end P&S have more settings than compact P&S. Understanding some of what's going on inside the camera helps you take better pictures, even if your camera doesn't enable you to control some of the settings in this Part.

For now, your most important task is to get to know your camera. Become familiar with how your camera works as you become more comfortable with the fundamentals of photography. Remember that you have no film to process, so get out there and push those buttons.

Understanding Exposure

Exposure refers to the amount of light allowed to fall on the image sensor in the camera during image capture. Exposure is the result of the combination of the length of time that the image sensor receives light *(shutter speed),* the size of the lens opening *(aperture),* and the light sensitivity of your image sensor *(ISO).* The next few sections tell you more about each of these settings.

Figure 5-1 shows the physical relationship of four hardware components. Light passes through the lens. The amount of light that enters the camera beyond the lens is controlled by the aperture. How long that aperture admits light is controlled by the shutter. Whatever light the aperture and shutter let in strikes the image sensor, whose sensitivity to that amount of light is modifiable. The image sensor translates light into digital information that is then written to your memory card.

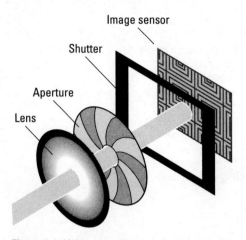

Figure 5-1: Light passes through the lens, aperture, and shutter to strike the image sensor.

Figure 5-2 represents the range between darker and lighter exposure. Each setting listed individually in the figure pushes exposure lighter or darker.

If you change just one of the three settings — say, shutter speed — you change the exposure. Increased shutter speed decreases exposure. That's ideal if the scene is very bright, but it isn't so good if the light is dim because there isn't enough time for the exposure. *Underexposure* translates into a darker image. Decreased shutter speed increases exposure, which is good for low light but washes out a photo in bright light. *Overexposure* translates into a lighter image.

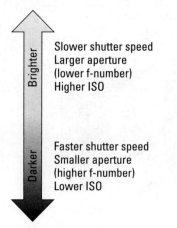

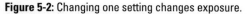

Figure 5-2: Changing one setting changes exposure.

Figure 5-3 shows an overexposed image (left) and an image that is underexposed (right). Notice the differences in details visible in the sky and in the hot air balloons (at Albuquerque International Balloon Fiesta in 2009).

 People react to photographs. Light affects mood and emotion. A bright scene may be uplifting; a dark scene may evoke somberness or look strikingly dramatic.

As you see in each of the following sections, your camera may let you control one variable while it adjusts the others. In terms of Figure 5-2, as you push a setting in one direction, the camera will push another setting in the other direction to try for balanced exposure. If your camera has a Manual mode, it enables you to change more than one setting and to choose a combination the camera might not choose. (Results can be good or bad, in any case.)

Overexposed

Underexposed

Photo credit: Merri Rudd

Figure 5-3: An overexposed image (top) and underexposed image (bottom).

Setting the shutter speed

The shutter has to open for any exposure to take place. That's why your camera has a shutter button, also called the shutter release, to trigger the opening of the shutter. How long the shutter remains open after you click that button is determined by the shutter speed setting. Outside on a sunny day, a faster shutter speed may be necessary to avoid overexposure. As the sun sets, you may want to use a slower shutter speed for the same level of exposure.

Shutter speeds are measured in fractions of seconds or whole seconds and usually range from 30 seconds (very slow) to ¼₀₀₀, or sometimes even ⅛₀₀₀, of a second (very fast). Some cameras also have a B (Bulb) mode, which enables you to keep the shutter open as long as you hold down the button.

On your camera's LCD or EVF, the shutter speed appears as a whole number like 800, but this is really a fraction of a second — 1/800.

Another consideration in setting shutter speed is whether anything in the scene is moving. When you're using slower shutter speeds and a stationary camera, objects in motion will blur. Higher shutter speeds freeze the action.

A camera's Sports mode automatically sets a higher shutter speed for action shots. Take advantage of that when photographing wildlife, too.

If your camera has Shutter Priority mode (most likely S or SP on the mode dial), use it to specify the shutter speed to use. In this mode, your camera automatically adjusts the aperture, which I discuss in the next section. When you choose a slower shutter speed, the exposure gets more time. Consequently, your camera automatically chooses a smaller aperture to admit less light for the exposure, avoiding overexposure. Conversely, choosing a faster shutter speed allows less time for the exposure, and your camera chooses a larger aperture to admit more light in the time available to avoid underexposure.

Keep the following in mind when you're setting shutter speed:

✔ **Set the shutter speed by turning the dial located on the front or top of your camera and looking at the LCD display.** On the Mode menu or dial, choose Shutter Priority mode, which may be labeled as S, SP, or Tv (as in *time value*). Setting your camera to Shutter Priority mode enables you to manually set the shutter speed while the camera determines all other settings. If you can't locate the dial, check your camera's user manual to see if your camera offers this mode.

 Look for an indicator in your EVF or on the LCD that confirms that the camera settings are within an approved programmed range. You may see a green light if the settings are acceptable or a red light if the settings are not acceptable.

✔ **Remember the light source.** The brighter the scene, the faster the shutter speed you can use, such as ¹⁄₄₀₀₀. For speeds slower than ¹⁄₆₀ of a second, you should use a tripod to avoid camera shake and to ensure a sharp image. If you don't have a tripod and your camera has an image-stabilization feature, be sure to turn it on for slower shutter speeds.

 When you use Shutter Priority mode, the aperture adjusts automatically. So, you don't have to worry about setting it manually.

> ✔ **Decide to blur or freeze the subject.** To inten-
> tionally blur an image with a moving subject
> *(motion blur),* set the shutter speed to a slower
> speed. To freeze the action in a shot, use a
> faster speed.

Figure 5-4 shows the blurring or motion effect possible with a slower shutter speed.

Photo credit: PhotoDisc

Figure 5-4: Set the shutter speed to a slower setting to blur an
image.

Figure 5-5 shows action stopped by a higher shutter speed.

Photo credit: Mark Justice Hinton

Figure 5-5: Set the shutter speed to a faster setting to freeze movement.

Changing the aperture

Like the pupil in your eye, a camera lens can open wide or be narrowed to the size of a pin prick. The lens opening is the aperture. A wide aperture lets in more light. A narrow aperture lets in less light. As you walk through a dark room, your pupil's aperture widens to let you see the dog that you're about to trip over. Flip on the light and your pupil's aperture narrows quickly to reduce the flood of light.

A bright scene might call for a narrower aperture, whereas a dimmer scene may need a wider aperture. When you use a scene mode such as Cloudy or Night

Sky, your camera chooses a wider aperture to let in more light because those are likely to be dimmer scenes. When you choose a beach or landscape scene mode, the camera automatically chooses a narrower aperture to reduce the light because those are likely to be bright scenes.

Another consideration is that aperture affects depth of field (DOF), the range in which objects are in focus. (Objects outside the DOF — both closer and farther than the subject of the photo — are out of focus.) The narrower the aperture, the deeper the DOF. The wider the aperture, the shallower the DOF.

Words like *narrower* or *shallower* seem vague until you fully appreciate the dimension or direction being discussed. Aperture is like a window. A narrow window lets in less light than a wide window. DOF is like a clear patch on a foggy road. The more of the road ahead you can see beyond your headlights, the deeper the DOF.

Not surprisingly, DOF conveys depth. Photography converts three dimensions into two. A deep DOF can emphasize distance. Figure 5-6 ranges from a nearby ruin (in Hovenweep National Monument, Utah), across a valley toward a distant mountain range. This is the deep DOF that comes from a small aperture.

You may want a shallow DOF to emphasize your subject by blurring objects in the background or foreground that distract. Figure 5-7 shows the shallow DOF that comes from a large aperture. The white apache plume flowers are in focus, but objects nearer and farther away are not.

Bokeh (from a Japanese word) is the term used to describe the out-of-focus area in a photo. Bokeh is considered an artistic effect.

Photo credit: Mark Justice Hinton

Figure 5-6: Small aperture; deep DOF — miles deep.

This is the tricky aspect of DOF. Focus is not just on a single point or plane in space. There is a range nearer and farther than the subject that is also in focus. If your DOF is 6 feet and your subject is 3 feet away, everything between you and the subject and 3 feet beyond is in focus. With the same depth of field and a subject that is 30 feet away, the effect is quite different. Consider Figure 5-6 again. Imagine if the valley were in focus but the ruins were not — that would be the case with a shallow DOF. Keep that same shallow DOF and focus on the ruins and nothing in the valley will be distinct.

On a cloudy day or in a room lit only by daylight coming through windows, you might need to widen the aperture to get enough exposure. However, that wider aperture reduces the DOF, increasing the odds that some part of the scene falls outside the focus and is blurry or fuzzy. That isn't necessarily bad — you can use that effect intentionally.

Photo credit: Mark Justice Hinton

Figure 5-7: Large aperture, shallow DOF.

Compact P&S cameras may not have an Aperture control (or Shutter Priority, for that matter), but scene modes vary aperture and, therefore, DOF.

Aperture is measured in *f-stops*. For example, f2.8 is a wide-open lens, admitting lots of light (with less DOF), whereas f8.0 is a narrow opening, admitting less light than f2.8 (but with greater DOF than f2.8). Every f-stop has a specific DOF associated with it.

Notice the paradox of f-stops: The higher the number, the narrower the aperture. That's because an f-stop is a ratio (hang in there) of the width of the lens opening to the focal length of the lens. Traditionally, f2.8 is written as *f/2.8;*

the lowercase *f* is the focal length and the aperture is the result of dividing the focal length of the lens by 2.8. As the f-stop number (the divisor, really) gets higher, the aperture gets narrower. An aperture of f4 (or f/4) divides the focal length by four. One-fourth is smaller than 1/2.8; f4 is narrower than f2.8; f8 is narrower still (1/8). With each step from f2.8 to f4 to f5.6 to f8, the aperture is narrower, admitting less light (and the DOF grows deeper with each step). See Figure 5-8 for graphic illustration of these differences.

Interestingly, each f-stop admits twice as much light as the next *higher* f-stop and half as much light as the next *lower* f-stop. (Relax, there won't be a quiz.)

If your camera has an Aperture Priority mode (usually an A or AP on the mode dial), use it to set the aperture you want and your camera automatically adjusts the shutter speed.

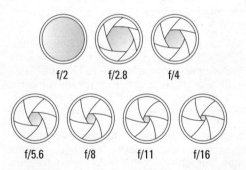

Figure 5-8: For aperture, bigger numbers mean smaller openings.

Shutter speed affects the freezing or blurring of moving objects within a scene.

All these details make you appreciate Automatic mode, don't they? But keep in mind that Automatic mode can't push the settings to change the mood or emphasize one part of the scene.

 Your LCD or EVF shows you whether the scene is brighter or darker as you adjust aperture. You won't see the effect on DOF, however. DSLRs may have a Preview button that shows DOF.

Keep these things in mind as you work with the aperture settings on your camera:

✔ **Set the aperture by turning the dial (located on the front or top) and looking at the LCD display.** On the Mode menu or dial, choose Aperture Priority mode, which may be labeled as A or Av (with the latter standing for *aperture value*). Setting your camera to Aperture Priority mode enables you to manually set the aperture while the camera determines all other settings. If you can't locate the dial, check your camera's user manual to see if your camera offers this mode.

 Look for an indicator in your EVF or on the LCD that the camera settings are within an approved programmed range. The indicator might be a green light (which means the settings are within range) or a red light (which means the settings are out of the approved range).

✔ **The brighter the scene, the narrower the aperture you can use, meaning a higher-numbered f-stop.** For wider apertures (lower-numbered f-stops), you should use a tripod to avoid camera shake and to ensure a sharp image. If you don't have a tripod and your camera has an image-stabilization feature, be sure to turn it on for wider apertures/lower f-stops.

When you use Aperture Priority the shutter speed adjusts automatically. Because a wide aperture admits more light, the camera will choose a faster shutter speed. With a smaller aperture admitting less light, the shutter speed slows. A slower shutter speed may result in blurring of objects moving in the picture.

Compensating with Exposure Value

There is another way to adjust exposure in small increments. Formally, this is called *exposure compensation* using *exposure values.* More simply, you adjust the current exposure using a control labeled EV or EC. This control works in any manual mode.

If you're lucky, your camera's EV control works in Auto mode, in which case it is the simplest way to make a photo lighter or darker without resorting to any other manual mode. If I could, I'd put a big star by this tip.

The EV control increases or decreases exposure as you adjust the control in a positive or negative direction. Recall that for any f-stop (aperture), one f-stop higher admits half as much light and one f-stop lower admits twice as much light. Fortunately, EV adjustments are usually in fractions of an f-stop, typically 1/3.

Try these steps:

1. **Locate your EV control (or EC).**

2. **In Auto mode, look for a zero on-screen (0E, 0EV, or 0EC).**

   If you don't see this information on-screen, switch to Aperture Priority or Shutter Priority.

3. **Move the EV control left or right, watching the EV information on screen.**

   You should see the number change anywhere from -3 to +3 (three full f-stops darker or lighter). Moreover, you should see the scene darken or lighten as you make this change.

4. **Shoot a photo of the sky with some puffy clouds or some leaves dappled with sun and shadow.**

   Take at least three shots of the same scene adjusting EV from negative to zero to positive. Compare these shots on your computer screen later.

Your camera remembers the EV setting until you switch modes or turn off the camera. Don't forget to manually switch back to 0EV before you take other photos.

DSLRs, like SLRs before them, accept filters on their lenses for various effects. One of these filters is a polarizer that aligns light as it enters the lens. One of the effects of a polarizing filter is deeper blue skies. You may find a similar effect in using EV to slightly underexpose the sky. (Polarizers also neutralize hazy skies, which EV won't do.)

Setting ISO

Before digital cameras, film was described as *fast* — very sensitive to light and fast to expose — or *slow* — less sensitive to light and slow to expose.

The standards for grading film's light sensitivity or *film speed* were established by the International Organization of Standards (ISO, an abbreviation taken from the French name of the organization). Although ISO is not a unit of measure, light sensitivity is graded in terms of ISO. Here, a bigger number indicates greater light sensitivity and faster exposure (and overexposure); a smaller number indicates less light sensitivity and slower exposure (or underexposure).

Although your digital camera doesn't use film, your camera's image sensor clearly is sensitive to light. And that sensitivity can be expressed as ISO.

Your camera has either a fixed ISO or chooses the ISO automatically based on conditions. You may be able to manually adjust the ISO. As you raise the ISO, you increase sensitivity — good for lower light. As you lower the ISO, you decrease sensitivity — good for normal or brighter light. Cameras often operate automatically around ISO 100 in most levels of daylight. ISO 1000 is very sensitive to light and might be appropriate for night shots with a tripod.

Vestiges of prior technology often carry forward into newer technology. What does clockwise mean anymore? Why do we still say that we dial our push-button phones? Likewise, ISO has been brought forward into the current age. This is not to say that ISO is archaic. ISO provides a transition from old to new.

The dark side of using high ISO film is the resulting texture of a photo. Exposures at higher ISO tend to be grainy, speckled, or uneven because the increased sensitivity of high ISO film comes from larger grains of silver halide. The smaller, finer grains of lower ISO film produce smoother images.

Although digital cameras aren't subject to the chemistry of film, high ISO still has problems. The increased sensitivity of a high ISO digital setting increases interference and degrades the sharpness of photos. This interference is called *noise.* Noise is especially noticeable as defects in enlargements. Higher ISO may be noisier than low ISO settings, much as higher ISO film is grainier than low ISO film.

The practical significance of ISO is not merely that you may be able to shoot in low light. Higher ISO increases light sensitivity and that makes available narrower apertures (greater DOF) or faster shutter speeds than would be possible with lower ISO at low light. Settings that would underexpose a given ISO setting will adequately expose a higher ISO. An added benefit is that you may be able to shoot in low light without a tripod.

Understandably, you want your photos to have good exposure — not too bright, not too dark. ISO, aperture, and shutter speed are interrelated in regard to exposure. You can achieve the same level of exposure with different combinations of these settings. One of those combinations might result in more or less DOF (aperture). Another might freeze or blur motion (shutter speed). Yet another combination might be more or less noisy, uneven, or grainy (ISO). The exposure might be the same in each of these instances, but your options are different.

In the various preset modes, such as Automatic or Night Sky, your camera selects an ISO setting according to the lighting in the shot, as well as the aperture and shutter speed.

Go ahead, change your ISO, if you have that option. Here are some things to think about as you play around with this setting:

- ✔ **Look around until you find the ISO option on your camera.** Because it's a less frequently adjusted setting, ISO may not be located with the other, more common options. (Basic cameras don't let you change the ISO setting.)

- ✔ **The lower the number of the ISO, the less sensitive your image sensor is to light.** A low ISO number results in a photo with very fine grain. An ISO setting of 100 is considered average, but a low ISO speed may not work in low-light scenarios. Normally, you want the lowest ISO setting possible for best quality, unless you want a grainy shot for creative reasons.

✔ **A high ISO number makes your image sensor more sensitive to light but may create a grainy, "noisy" image.** High ISO settings may be necessary in low-light situations, especially when you're using a faster shutter speed, a narrower aperture, or both — for example, when you're shooting a moving subject inside a building without using a flash.

✔ **As with the other settings, you should take several similar shots, varying just the ISO setting.** You may not be able to see any difference on your LCD. You're more likely to see differences on a computer screen.

Part VI

Ten Tips for Better Photos and Videos

● ●

*B*efore you begin shooting pictures, a few simple steps can ensure that your photos and videos turn out as well as they can. After you've taken the shot, some simple edits can improve photos even more. This Part provides ten easy tips for taking better photographs and videos.

Know Your Camera

To take pictures, all you really have to know is how to turn the camera on and confirm it is in Automatic mode. However, your camera is capable of much more, even if you don't use all of its features. Beyond the topics covered elsewhere in this book, here are six more features to look for and adjustments you can make on your camera:

- ✔ Turn off digital zoom to avoid pixilation (jagged dots).

- ✔ Turn on image stabilization to avoid blurring.

- ✔ Turn off automatic flash to avoid unexpected flashes that may startle your subject. Automatic flash may go off pointlessly in landscapes or when using the zoom or macro feature.

- ✔ Turn on flash when the scene is bright but the subject is in shadow or lit from behind (*force* or *fill flash*).

- ✔ Use exposure compensation to push a photo lighter or darker.

- ✔ Use white balance to compensate for fluorescent, incandescent, and other tinted light sources.

Become One with Your Camera

The camera does you no good if you leave it somewhere else. Take your camera with you. Don't be afraid to look like a tourist or a camera geek. And the camera does you no good if it's turned off. Have the lens cap off, the camera on and in hand, and be ready for the next great photo.

Even so, practice discretion. People may not want you to photograph them, so be considerate. Point your camera down when you're not taking pictures. Ask for permission to take photos of people you don't know. Flowers and animals, on the other hand, seldom object to being in photos.

Use a Tripod

A tripod is a must for shooting under low light or with some longer lenses. A tripod is also quite handy for self portraits and group portraits. You may want a full-size tripod, but everyone needs a pocket-size version at a minimum. selecting a tripod, look for one that is easy to adjust and which feels steady.

For videos, a tripod reduces distracting camera movements. Good tripods let you pan smoothly left, right, up, or down.

Change Your Perspective

Move around as much as you can under the circumstances. Try crouching for shorter or lower subjects. Try holding the camera over your head to clear a crowd. (A tiltable LCD is very helpful in such cases.) Move left and right of the subject to try different angles. You'll discover interesting facets of the subject and new angles on the light. Photograph flowers up close with the light source behind them for interesting color and details. In Figure 6-1, the cosmos blossom on the left is seen from the front, whereas the shot on the right is from behind, revealing the translucent nature of flowers (and leaves).

Figure 6-1: Change your perspective to reveal insights into your subject.

If you move while taking videos, do so very slowly. This includes panning and zooming in and out — go slowly.

Take Lots of Pictures

Aside from your initial investment for the camera, digital photos essentially cost you nothing. Go wild. Don't take just a few photos, take dozens. Don't come back from vacation with 50 photos; come back with 500 — you just need to remember to pack enough memory cards to fit 500 photos, if you don't plan to move photos from camera to computer as you go. Examine your photos for new ideas or mistakes in composition and exposure.

This liberation comes with an obligation: Don't expect anyone to look at every picture you take, no matter how much they love you. Before you show your photos to friends and family, select the better ones for show and skip (or delete) the less interesting ones. If you have five cool shots of a scene, pick the best, and maybe the second best, to show.

Be Quiet

If you're shooting videos, avoid making distracting sounds or engaging in distracting conversations (or monologues, as the case may be). Let people know when you're shooting video or "what'cha doin'?" could end up on the sound track. Keep in mind other noises such as wind and traffic you might tune out but that could spoil a video.

Being quiet matters in taking photos, too, especially with wildlife or candid shots.

Keep It Short

Videos produce large files that take up lots of storage space, as well as the time it takes to copy large files to your computer. Consider your audience: Do they want to sit through 20 minutes of a kid in a sandbox? Keep most videos short — under a couple of minutes, rarely over five minutes.

Back Up Your Files

It should be a given with all digital data that you have a plan for frequent and regular backups. (Odds are you don't. No show of hands here.) There are many different schemes for backup — from full backups of the entire computer to selective backups of individual folders or files. The question is: What will you do when you change your mind about an edit or deletion? Move your files from the camera to the computer and back them up before you begin deleting or editing. Then back them up again after you've carefully organized, edited, and tagged them.

Learn to Edit

You can perform the most basic editing functions with tools you may already have or that you can download from the Web for free. These essential edits include rotating, cropping, and resizing photos. Much more sophisticated editing allows you to tweak individual pixels and completely transform a photo. Start with the basics and move on to fancier tasks when you're ready.

Figure 6-2 shows the original photo of a praying mantis on the left. The background is distracting (and

irrelevant) and the tilted post is, too. The cropped
and straightened photo appears on the right of
Figure 6-2.

Figure 6-2: Simple edits can greatly improve some photos.

Share and Participate

If you like your photos, someone else will, too. Share
your photos a few at a time by e-mail or in larger
batches through a Web-based photo or video sharing
site. (Don't e-mail videos, just upload them.) Give
back to your community by looking at other people's
photos and commenting appropriately. Everyone
wants his or her photos to be seen.